ENGLISH LANGUAGE IN INDIA

This book examines the relationship between the English language and growth – economic and inclusive – in India. It explores why English continues to be the language of aspiration long after Independence. With the second largest English-speaking population in the world today, India is a testament to how a linguistic legacy continues to cast a long shadow on its contemporary discourse in the economic arena.

This volume:

- Explores how English language proficiency constitutes as human capital.
- Draws on the latest India Human Development Survey data.
- Investigates the relationship between the language and economic indicators such as wages, household income and state growth.
- Further investigates the role of the English language in the inclusivity of growth.
- Provides a snapshot on the pedagogy of English in the Indian education system.

The first of its kind in scope, this volume will be of great interest to scholars of economics, education, sociolinguistics, development studies, politics and sociology. It will also be of great interest to the general reader.

Jaskiran Bedi has a PhD in Development Studies from the University of Cambridge, UK. She is currently working as a Fellow under the Chief Minister's Urban Leaders Fellowship, New Delhi, India. Prior to this, she pursued an MPhil in Development Studies from the University of Cambridge and a BSc (Hons) degree in Philosophy, Politics, Economics (PPE) from the University of Warwick. Her area of academic research within the development domain concentrates on labour and education economics – particularly, the role of language as human capital and its subsequent impact. She has also worked with several public and private sector agencies, including Ernst & Young, the Department for International Development, Oxfam and the International Labour Organisation.

"Jaskiran Bedi has written a path-breaking study on the role of language in development. This is an extremely important but greatly under-researched topic. English language has essentially become the language of globalisation. Use of the English language is potentially of great importance in relation to economic and social development. Arguably, its significance in developing countries has increased as the role of global services has expanded. India is a wonderful case study to use for research into this topic. It is especially interesting because the penetration of the English language in India is far less than is commonly thought to be the case. Dr Bedi's study makes use of highly original fieldwork and provides valuable insights for both scholars and policy-makers."

—Peter Nolan, Founding Director of the University of Cambridge's Centre of Development Studies, Emeritus Chong Hua Professor in Chinese Development, and Director of the Chinese Executive Leadership Programme (CELP)

"This is a riveting analysis of the history, politics and economics of the English language in India. Based on survey data and statistical analysis, it shows that knowing English has large economic payoffs in the labour market, making it a source of economic inequality. The author considers many aspects and offers policy directions. High quality scholarship presented in an engaging, accessible manner."

—Geeta Gandhi Kingdon, Chair of Education Economics and International Development, Institute of Education, University College London

"This volume is innovative in its objective of bringing language learning into the field of the economics of education. A commendable range of views: from the history of the English language, to the implications of English learning on economic growth, and the challenge of inclusivity. The careful balance between primary research and secondary analysis will make it invaluable to academics and policy-makers."

—Shailaja Fennell, University of Cambridge Senior Lecturer in Development Studies and Director of Research at Cambridge Central Asia Forum

ENGLISH LANGUAGE IN INDIA

A Dichotomy Between Economic Growth and Inclusive Growth

Jaskiran Bedi

Routledge
Taylor & Francis Group
LONDON AND NEW YORK

First published 2020
by Routledge
2 Park Square, Milton Park, Abingdon, Oxon OX14 4RN

and by Routledge
605 Third Avenue, New York, NY 10017

First issued in paperback 2021

Routledge is an imprint of the Taylor & Francis Group, an informa business

Publisher's Note
The publisher has gone to great lengths to ensure the quality of this reprint but points out that some imperfections in the original copies may be apparent.

British Library Cataloguing-in-Publication Data
A catalogue record for this book is available from the British Library

Library of Congress Cataloging-in-Publication Data
A catalog record for this book has been requested

ISBN 13: 978-0-367-65503-7 (pbk)
ISBN 13: 978-1-138-38457-6 (hbk)
ISBN 13: 978-0-429-32832-9 (ebk)

DOI: 10.4324/9780429328329

Typeset in Sabon
by Apex CoVantage, LLC

To my grandmother, Prof Ajit Singh, Giulio and Tammy,
You are missed.

To mum and dad,
Thank you.

CONTENTS

List of figures viii
List of tables ix
Acknowledgements xi

1 Introduction 1

2 History of the English language in India 9

3 The English language and economic growth 42

4 The English language and inclusive growth 86

5 The Indian education system 109

6 Conclusion 138

Appendices 141
Bibliography 155

FIGURES

3.1	Relationship between English language and economic growth	45
4.1	Relationship between English language and inclusive growth	90
4.2	Indian income pyramid	93
4.3	IHSD-Round 2 sample disaggregated by household income level (2011)	93
4.4	Percentage of individuals in deprived households segregated by English ability (2011)	95
5.1	Sample profile – gender (CBSE)	118
5.2	Sample profile – school management (CBSE)	118
5.3	Percentage of students stating English proficiency (CBSE)	121
5.4	Self-assessment of English proficiency	125
5.5	School management of CBSE students stating inability to speak and express in English	125
5.6	Two-tiered process for improved English learning	133
A4.1	Sample profile – gender	145
A4.2	Sample profile – social group	146
A4.3	Sample profile – residence	147
A4.4	Sample profile – SSLC exam performance	148
A4.5	Sample profile – failed/repeated a grade	148

TABLES

2.1 Timeline of key events leading to English language implementation in India 11
2.2 Percentage of English speakers in India in 2005 and 2011 31
2.3 Distribution of India's GDP by sector 35
3.1 Percentage of English speakers in India (2011) 51
3.2 Percentage of English speakers distributed by states 53
3.3 Effect of English speaking ability on log hourly wages 57
3.4 Effect of English speaking ability on log hourly wages 62
3.5 Returns to English-speaking skills – household heads 66
3.6 Returns to English-speaking skills – male household heads (2011) 68
3.7 Returns to English-speaking skills by sector (2011) 70
3.8 Growth Rate of GSDP of sectors at constant 2004–2005 Prices 80
3.9 Relationship between English language and the growth rate of GSDP segregated by sectors 81
4.1 Percentage of English speakers segregated by annual household income (2011) 94
4.2 Regression of English ability on the probability of moving out of deprivation 96
4.3 Average annual earnings and percentage of non-English speakers (managers in wholesale/retail versus assemblers) 101
4.4 Average annual earnings and percentage of non-English speakers (technology engineers versus printers) 101
4.5 Qualitative responses pertaining to the importance of English language as a criterion of employment and higher postings 103
4.6 Average annual earnings and percentage of non-English speakers (managers versus back-office staff) 104
4.7 Effects of English speaking ability on the probability of sector employment 105

4.8	Average annual earnings and percentage of non-English speakers by occupation (service sector)	105
5.1	Mark scheme for student test	117
5.2	Overall average marks and English marks obtained by CBSE students in Grade 10 board examinations	119
5.3	Average overall marks obtained by CBSE students in Grade 10 board examinations segregated by school management	120
5.4	English subject marks obtained by CBSE students in Grade 10 board examinations segregated by school management	120
5.5	Percentage of CBSE students with reading and comprehension skills	122
5.6	Overall average marks and English marks obtained by IB students in Grade 10 IGCSE examinations	124
5.7	Percentage of students with reading and comprehension skills – known script	127
5.8	Percentage of students with reading and comprehension skills – unknown script	127
5.9	Major challenges faced by CBSE students while learning English	130
A1	Timeline of key events of East India Company's annexation of India	141
A2	Services sectors included in the 2008 National Industrial Classification	143
A3	Percentage of English speakers distributed by states	144
A4.1	Sample profile – religion	146
A4.2	Sample profile – years of schooling completed	147
A5	Returns to English skills on log hourly wages in non-agriculture primary sector by age (2011)	149

ACKNOWLEDGEMENTS

Academic writing can be an arduous task. Penning down and substantiating an idea takes passion, time and effort on the part of the writer. However, for the idea to be seeded, elaborated and effectively communicated, a solid support structure is a required blessing. I, therefore, extend my acknowledgement to all the people who added their wisdom, thoughts and support to my work and played their significant role in keeping me going.

The foundation of this structure is my family. To begin with, I must, with all my heart, thank my parents for the faith they have displayed in me. They raised me to believe that the quest for knowledge is never a futile task, and they invested heavily in my pursuit of it. The preliminary idea of this work, my ability to translate that to written words, the resources required for substantiation – are all to their credit. I must also thank my brother Sanjay and my sister Simran and their respective partners (Shipra and Nihaal) for their consistent support. Their words of encouragement became the prerequisite pillars of this study. Here's to hoping that my baby nephew and niece read this book two decades later and find it interesting.

I extend my gratitude to my PhD supervisor, Dr Shailaja Fennell, for always being available to deal with my doubts and panic attacks – even after graduation. Regardless of the quantum of work she had, she ensured sufficient time allocation for thought-provoking discussions. This research would not have seen the light of day without her support.

I thank late Prof Ajit Singh and Ann Zammit for being an inspiration and for ingraining in me dedication. Equally important are the brilliant academics who inspired my work either through their teachings during MPhil or through their relevant inputs and/or feedback on my research during the PhD – (in alphabetical order) Dr Gay Meeks, Prof Geeta Kingdon, Dr Ha-Joon Chang, Dr Michael Kuczynski and Prof Peter Nolan.

I would like to thank each and every member of the Centre of Development Studies, University of Cambridge. Every discussion and meeting – formal or over a glass of wine – paved way for scholarly ideations that subsequently played a huge role in moulding my thesis – which became the frame of this book. It was a privilege being a part of a group so intellectually advanced.

This book would have been incomplete had it not been for the works of the scholars and writers I have cited and referenced. They provided the base, underpinning and validation to my arguments. A big thank you must also be said to all the persons – students, teachers, employers, employees – who took out the time to fill in the surveys and interact with me for this work. Without them, this work would have been nothing but a mere opinion.

A heartfelt gratitude must also be extended to the faculty, staff and students of Newham College and Lucy Cavendish College (thank you for being a home away from home), University of Warwick (thank you for paving and moulding my academic interest) and Pathways World School (thank you for nurturing me into who I am).

Finally, I would like to thank Routledge – Taylor & Francis, particularly Aakash Chakrabarty and Brinda Sen, for recognising this research and giving it the platform to reach a wider audience.

I

INTRODUCTION

The unexplored link

Language.

Take a moment to think about the concept, and what it means in your life. Now, define it.

Did you describe it as a method of human communication? Perhaps a medium of social interaction? Or did you take a more linguistic approach and think of it as understandable utterances and sounds? Perhaps you thought philosophically and dwelled into the ontologies?

Take another moment and deconstruct what made you reach your definition. Particularly, what aspects of your life struck you when deducing your description of "language?"

When I ask this question, generally and broadly, the answers I receive are along the lines of education, social surroundings and work. Indeed, language is the medium of sharing knowledge, our day to day interactions with society and our communication at work. However, what if you're put in a school where you don't know the language of teaching, or a society where you don't know the language of preference, or a workplace where you don't know the language of transaction? What is the concept of "language" to you then?

A man named Giri from a rural village of Rajasthan in India defined "language" as a medium of discrimination. This description highlights that contemplation on the links between language and development is well overdue.

A discussion on the said link ensued in the seventh Language and Development Conference held in Addis Ababa in 2005. Debating on the role of languages in the domain of education, experts at this conference pressed on African countries to reinstate their local languages so as to achieve socio-economic growth. Education consultant John Clegg famously stated that "you can't learn if you don't understand lessons and you can't teach if you're not confident in the language of learning," emphasising that language policies that promote the use of a non-mother-tongue (often English) as the medium of instruction could be working against education attainment in Africa, hence hindering development in the region.[1] Understandably, this came as a shock to many, as today's common belief dictates that children who start learning in the global languages as early as possible are inevitably advantaged nationally and globally. Regardless of the belief held by the audience, from this debate, it became clear to all that better understanding of the impact of language on development should become a high priority for policy-makers.

This book is an attempt to further the nascent discussions on the language-development link, shifting the geographical focus to the Indian context. Given the diversity of global languages[2] and the breadth of the concept of development,[3] it will be ambitious and foolish of me to not circumscribe the two. The geographical context of this book as well as other reasons (discussed in the subsequent chapters), cull out English language and growth (economic and inclusive) as the fathomable focus areas. This book, as a literal elongation of its title, will provide observations on the paradoxical relationships between the English language and growth in India.

Prior to starting, however, I make the following set of disclaimers that readers must note.

1 The relationship of a language on economic growth and development is different for different countries since its implications are through factors including diffusion of knowledge and promotion of trade for the former and through institutions including educational, political, legal and administrative for the latter. For instance, while English can act as a lingua franca in the European Union without hampering the region's development conditions, it can be a marker of elite status, and ergo a discriminatory factor, in India and Africa given its dominant position in government and higher education.
2 The consequence of language on development is further determined by added variables such the diversity of the zone, diversity of languages and the origin of the diverse languages. For instance, though the economic zones of both Europe and India prosper from economic growth arising from English proficiency,[4] yet unlike the multilingual EU, the multilingual India might suffer from inequality of English-speaking skills, perpetuating into inequality of income. This could, perhaps, stem from the fact that English borrows largely from Latin, the mother tongue of various European Languages, while most Indian languages, including Hindi, originate from Sanskrit, hence making it easier for non-English European speakers to fathom the language relative to non-English Indian speakers. Moreover, the colonial legacy of English in India gives it a special elite status in this specific country. Therefore, the use of non-mother-tongue English is not a universal hindrance to development.
3 Furthermore, prominent usage of non-mother-tongue English can affect different facets of development differently. For instance, though legitimising socio-economic class disparities in India, English has deterred

> marginalisation of smaller language groups that Hindi could have stirred had it been proclaimed the sole national language of India. In doing so, the English language has pacified and prevented civil conflicts. The language has also made political administration easier in this diverse multilingual country by bridging the communication between the linguistically varying regions.

Evidently, the degree and facets of development that are affected by the English language vary in different contexts. Therefore, readers must keep in mind that this particular book is based solely on the unique case of India, and the particular facet of development it concentrates on is growth – both economic and inclusive.

English: the global language

> *The British Empire may be in full retreat with the handover of Hong Kong. But from Bengal to Belize and Las Vegas to Lahore, the language of the sceptred isle is rapidly becoming the first global lingua franca.*
>
> – (Globe and Mail, 1997)

Before I discuss the economic effects of the English language in India, I must highlight why I have chosen to study this particular language. The reason stems from the introductory quote of the chapter. The statement, written in *Globe and Mail*'s 1997 article titled "English Rules," has been famously cited by the renowned linguist, academic and author David Crystal in his book *English as a Global Language*.[5] Crystal highlighted it not simply for its alliterative ingenuity but also because of its implicative suggestion that the English language is universal and is here to stay. This implication is evident everywhere we turn today. Simply log on to your internet and type "Global Language" on your search engine. The word "English" will populate your screen, and how!

The commonly accepted perception of the universality of the English language is the reason for my inclination to explore it. Not everyone in this world speaks the language. Not every country in this world gives it a national or native language status. Yet we have people (some, if not all) in every country speaking the language. The dissemination of the language, in terms of spread, cannot be argued against. It is of interest to analyse how this global occurrence, which might or might not get further embedded in the global infrastructure, affects individual countries like India at present.

How the English language gained a universal status has been discussed in numerous newspaper articles, blogs, academic journals and books. Most publications on the topic have propagated their own unique story to explain the rise and spread of English. Their predictive implications about the sustainability and future of the language also differ. While some say English is here to stay,[6] others state that other languages may take over,[7] and English may fragment into a family of languages.[8] However, every narrative agrees on and credits two historical events as the providers of the predominant thrust to the language's journey to universality – Britain's political expansion and the United States of America's economic expansion.

Though the language came into existence in the fifth century with patterns of people movement and resettlement, it was in the nineteenth century that Britain consolidated the global position of English with its distinctive mix of trade and cultural politics. Thus came about the initial creation of a "language on which the sun never sets."[9] What added to the spread was the emergence of the United States as the economic power in the twentieth century, aided by the era of globalisation. In other words, while Great Britain steered the *introduction* of English to the world at large through their imperialist expansion, the United States ensured the *prevalence* of the language by dominating the economic arena since the twentieth century.

These two historical events paved the way for a world which, according to linguist Braj Kachru, can be viewed as concentric circles. Each circle represents the different way in which the English language has been historically acquired and used.

At its core, we have the *inner circle*, which encompasses countries such as the UK, Ireland, USA, Canada, New Zealand and Australia, where English is the primary language. This is followed by the *outer* or *extended circle*, which constitutes the non-native countries where English is important because of the aforementioned historical reasons. These countries have, over the years, entrenched the language in their institutional infrastructure and have chief institutions dependent on English. As a result, English has been granted a special "second language" role in these nations, which are predominantly multilingual. India, along with over 50 countries including Pakistan, Bangladesh, Singapore, Malaysia, Philippines, Tanzania, Nigeria, Kenya, etc., falls in this circle. Finally, we have the *expanding* or *extending circle*, which involves countries that recognise the importance of English as a global language and therefore use it as a foreign language but have no history of colonisation by members of the inner circle. This circle accounts for much of the rest of the world's population, including China, Japan, Korea, Indonesia, Egypt and most of Europe.

Noteworthy publications exist on the chronological movement of the English language from the *inner circle* to the *outer* and *expanding* circles,[10] thereby highlighting that English has indeed become the global language. What now needs to be explored is the *within-country* spread and usage of English in the *outer* and *expanding* circles. In the countries of these circles, how has the English language disseminated internally? What is the degree of this dissemination? What internal factors are enabling the scale-up? How is this foreign language getting consolidated despite the existence of other native and indigenous languages? Most importantly, how is this globally important language locally affecting the people? Does the global language requirement have a paradoxical relationship with the local language requirement? If yes, what should policy-makers of these countries do? It is fathomably fascinating to think about these within-country questions, and this book looks into exploring the local effects of a global phenomenon.

Why India?

> *In the classic Odia short story of the late 19th Century called "Daka Munshi," Fakir Mohan Senapati's memorable character, Gopal Babu, the English educated postmaster, treats his father Hari Singh as a "fool" and an "imbecile," showering upon him gratuitous "English blows" for his ignorance of English.*
>
> – (Sachidananda Mohanty, 2012)

Fakir Mohan Senapati was a renowned nineteenth-century writer, regarded as the father of modern Odia literature. His short story, titled "Daka Munshi," highlighted the debate over the English language and its selective appropriation by the elites in India during the colonial era. What needs to be noted here is that Senapati's described social realism, pertaining to discrimination caused by the English language, was set in the colonial backdrop.

Cut to 2012, when Sachidananda Mohanty, professor of English at the University of Hyderabad, referred to "Daka Munshi" to repeat the point that Senapati was making, equating the thrust of the English language with the British colonising agenda.[11] The fact that he used a nineteenth-century reference in the twenty-first century is a comment on the persistence of the role of the language. In doing so, Mohanty, while stressing on the importance of multilingualism, extended the language-related social realism of Senapati's time to contemporary India.

Cut to 2017, when a popular Bollywood movie named *Hindi Medium* released to significant accolades. In the acclaimed movie, the protagonist, post English-speaking attempts to get his daughter admitted to a "good" primary school, exasperatedly says, "***India is English, English is India.***" Professional critics lauded the movie for dealing with "a very relevant subject of how language divides our society."[12] The audience reviews on Google embedded the professional opinions, with one member writing, "*Hindi Medium* isn't a movie. It is reality." A follow-up response by a fellow commenter added, "What has been shown is not the reality. Reality is worse."

The common wisdom, jotted down and reiterated for wider consumption by the popular media since the colonial era, has time and again highlighted the dominant role of the English language in India. Literature, movies, newspaper articles and so on have consistently voiced a perception that has been engrained in all Indians – the English language is elite and important, and damned are those who are not well-versed in it. This superiority credited to English not only makes the language a mark of status, but also enables it to carry a strong hold on other socio-economic domains of India. Today, English has become an essential criterion for prosperity, knowledge and, at times, basic survival in the country.

Whether it is a road sign, a name plate, a medicine label, packaged food or officiating government documents, the content is almost always in English. While higher education is conducted entirely in English, the consumer demand at the primary and secondary levels is for the language. The rationale for this demand, consistent from Kangra to Karur, stems from the opinion that English proficiency will subsequently perpetuate into a well-paying job. Hindustan Pencil's company director stated that "a villager has more respect for a brand that is written in English" to justify printing the brand name, "Jobber," in English on its low cost pencils that are sold to rural children.[13] Google India's vice president, despite boldly stating that "English is over," conceded that while 90% of net users in India are non-English speaking, there is "not enough (local language) content which is being created right now."[14]

The truth is that English has become the de facto national language of India, despite the existence of fervent sentiments promoting the enhancement of indigenous languages. This superior status allocated to the language, particularly in the education and economic domains, is an intriguing topic of discussion for three reasons.

First, *the majority of the Indian population does not know English*. Only 259,000 Indians, out of 1.21 billion, reported English as their primary language in the 2011 Census, facing a decadal increase of 15%. Compared to this, the number of primary Hindi speakers was as high as 521 million, facing a decadal increase of 25%. Triangulation (which will be presented in detail in the following chapters) of the recently published India Human Development Survey Round II data shows that as of 2011, a mere 6% of Indians stated they could speak English fluently. Evidently, English speakers in India are limited in number. The proportion of people who can both speak and write English will presumably be lower. In comparison, Hindi-speakers are near the majority of the nation's population. Yet, it is English, rather than Hindi, that is given supervalent importance as a criterion for employment, medium for effective transactional communication, and symbol of superior knowledge and education.

Second, *English is just one of the many languages in the multilingual India*. The 1991 census recognised 1,576 classified "mother tongues." The

People of India Project of Anthropological Survey of India (2008) reported 325 languages, which are used for in-group communication by the Indian communities. More recently, the 2011 census identified 1,369 rationalised mother tongues. Classification of the 1,369 rationalised mother tongues, following linguistic methods for rational grouping based on available linguistic information, yielded a total number of 121 languages. The People's Linguistic Survey of India (2016) reported the existence of 780 living languages in India and potentially another 100 unreported languages. Ethnologue, as of 2019, listed 447 living languages in India. With so many options, it is intriguing that India still depends on a western language that is unknown to the majority of its population to such an elevated degree.

Third, despite the huge popularity of the topic in the media, *very little research has been done addressing the interlinkages between the Indian economy and the English language*. Literature focusing on India's growth has not comprehensively addressed market imperfections that hinder the positive correlation between education and growth, both economic and inclusive, in India. The unequal distribution of English-speaking skills as a market imperfection has not been analysed in any previous research. Literature focusing on the impact of the English language in India has limited its scope to the social and psychological fields.[15] The perpetuation of language inequality into the economic field has not been thoroughly considered.

Despite being one of the many languages and spoken only by a few, the English language has an under-researched yet evident grasp on the Indian economy and education sectors. A common Indian citizen is aware that the "good" schools and colleges of India are English focused, and the job market in India (may it be the private sector or the public sector) predominantly requires English-speaking capability. The media highlights that the importance attributed to the language might disadvantage the non-English speakers at the education level and labour market, paving the way for class distinction. When one contrasts this picture with China, where people prosper from economic, social and practical incentives by being functional in Putonghua, the explanation for the socio-economic class divide and the lack of inclusive growth in India might get a new linguistic explanation.

It is with the aim to explore this new potential explanation that I have opted for the Indian context. How did this western language become embedded in the Indian economic infrastructure? Has the multilingual India's dependence on the English language in its job market paved the way for positive returns due to English skills? If yes, to what extent? By extension, has India's dependence on the language in the economic sphere created a dichotomy between economic growth and the inclusivity of that growth, given the limited population with proficiency? What is this global language's future in the Indian economy – and is it here to stay?

Notes

1 In Coleman, H. (Ed.). (2007). *Language and development: Africa and beyond.* Addis Ababa: British Council Ethiopia. The full chapter can be retrieved from www.langdevconferences.org/publications/2005-AddisAbabaEthiopia/Chapter%204%20-%20Moving%20towards%20bilingual%20education%20in%20Africa-John%20Clegg.pdf
2 As of July 2018, there are 7,097 living languages in the world as per Ethnologue (2018). Languages of the World Retrieved July 14, 2018, from www.ethnologue.com
3 I thoroughly prescribe by Amartya Sen's concept of "Development as Freedom" (1999), which expands development beyond economic growth. It brings into its purview freedom from poverty, tyranny, poor economic opportunities, systematic social deprivation, neglect of public facilities and intolerance or over activity of repressive states.
4 Lee, C. G. (2012). English language and economic growth: Cross-country empirical evidence. *Journal of Economic and Social Studies*, *2*(1), 5–20.
5 Globe and Mail (1997) article cited in Crystal, D. (2003). *English as global language.* New York: Cambridge University Press.
6 Crystal, D. (2003). *English as global language.* New York: Cambridge University Press.
7 Graddol, D. (2007). *The future of English?* London: The British Council.
8 McArthur, T. (1998). *The English languages.* Cambridge: Cambridge University Press.
9 Graddol, *The future of English?*
10 To get the details on how English became the global language, I recommend Crystal, D. (2003). *English as a global language.* New York: Cambridge University Press. It takes a historical narrative approach to examine the factors that have led to the current position of English.
11 *The Hindu.* (2012, October 13). *English language learning must go hand in hand with multilingualism.* Retrieved August 9, 2018, from www.thehindu.com/todays-paper/tp-opinion/english-language-learning-must-go-hand-in-hand-with-multilingualism/article12556298.ece
12 *The Times of India.* (2017, May 25). *Hindi medium movie review.* Retrieved August 9, 2018, from https://timesofindia.indiatimes.com/entertainment/hindi/movie-reviews/hindi-medium/movie-review/58716386.cms
13 Joseph, M. (2011, February 16). India faces a linguistic truth: English spoken here. *The New York Times.* Retrieved August 12, 2018, from www.nytimes.com/2011/02/17/world/asia/17iht-letter17.html
14 *The Times of India.* (2017, April 26). *90% of the new net owners non-English.* Retrieved August 12, 2018, from https://timesofindia.indiatimes.com/business/india-business/90-of-new-net-users-non-english/articleshow/58371769.cms
15 For the functions of English in India from socio-psychological and political perspectives, see Agnihotri and Khanna (1997) and Brass (1974) respectively.

2

HISTORY OF THE ENGLISH LANGUAGE IN INDIA

The origin

I have never found one among them who could deny that a single shelf of a good European library was worth more than the whole native literature of India and Arabia. The intrinsic superiority of the Western literature is indeed fully admitted by those members of the committee who support the oriental plan of education.

– (Thomas Babington Macaulay, 1835)[1]

The heritage of the English language in India is relevant, as it provides the background to the supervalent importance given to the language in the country, which in turn goes a long way to explain why it has such an eminent role – both detrimental and favourable – in India relative to other developing countries. It is with this rationale that I present an overview of the historical and contemporary picture of the language in India.

David Crystal propagated that a language gains dominance primarily due to the political and military power of its native people.[2] Keeping this view in mind, all the global literature on the English language attributed the spread of the language to British colonial expansion. India was no exception, as Britain's colonial conquest of the country brought along with it the use of the western language. In its essence, colonialism refers to "the state of inferiority or of servitude experienced by a community, country or a nation dominated politically, economically and culturally by a more developed nation."[3] It was this economic, political and cultural domination by English-speaking Britain that brought about the introduction of the foreign language in India.

Britain first entered the subcontinent through the East India Company, which established traction in India with the development of a factory in Masulipatnam (in the current state of Andhra Pradesh), in 1611. This was followed by a grant of the rights provided by the then Mughal Emperor Jahangir, to establish a factory in Surat (now in Gujarat) in 1612. The company's victory in the 1757 Battle of Plassey and 1764 Battle of Buxar consolidated its power. Through these victorious battles, the Company forced the then Mughal Emperor, Shah Alam II, to appoint it the revenue collector, or *diwan*, of Bengal, Bihar and Orissa. The Indian subcontinent finally came under the direct rule of the Crown, or the British *Raj*, in 1858.

One might debate over whether British political rule in India was a simple foreign rule,[4] paternalistic benevolence, the "white man's burden,"[5] training Indian towards self- government,[6] exploitative and regenerative[7] or a "*trimurti* of *sarkar*, *sahukar* and *zamindar*."[8] However, there are two facts that are undisputed:

1 Regardless of the reason or justification for the political control, Britain required a common official language with the Indians (or a tier of Indians) to have effective trade and governance.
2 Many British officials believed that India was becoming decadent and only western education and knowledge could revitalise it.

In its preliminary phase, the company used Indian languages to communicate with and govern the masses. Moreover, it maintained publications and supported education in the native Sanskrit (in *Gurukulas*), and Persian and Arabic (in *Madrasas*). Indeed, the first Governor General of India from 1773 to 1785, Warren Hastings, encouraged Englishmen to familiarise themselves with Indian languages and culture to blend in. However, Britain soon realised that the solution to their objectives of governing the masses as well as reviving the decadent India relied on one factor – the English language. Educating a tier of Indians in English would not only aid and ease the governance of India, but it would also enable the Indians to learn the perceived superior European culture and knowledge. Therefore, Britain's inclination towards the introduction of the English language in India gained momentum gradually, and the ultimate leap towards the western language took place in 1835 with the English Education Act.

Extensive and rich literature is available that covers, in detail, the introduction of the English language in India. A seminal work that I rely on is Suresh Chandra Ghosh's 1995 paper titled "Bentinck, Macaulay and the Introduction of English Education in India."[9] Through a comprehensive historical investigation and literature review, Ghosh propagates that three individuals were responsible, explicitly or otherwise, for India's shift to the English language: Charles Grant, Thomas Babington Macaulay and William Bentinck. To this, I add a fourth catalyst – James Mill. While Macaulay and Bentinck became the immediate drivers of India's shift towards the English language, it was Grant and Mill's opinions on the subject that gave the preliminary thrust. Though I present in this chapter a quick recap of the academically accepted occurrences, starting with a timeline summarising the key events (see Table 2.1), I urge readers to consult Ghosh's paper for a detailed narrative on Grant, Macaulay and Bentinck.

Table 2.1 Timeline of key events leading to English language implementation in India

1767	Charles Grant, an official of the East India Company, arrives in India.
1790	Charles Grant returns to England and starts writing his treatise titled "Observations on the state of society among the Asiatic subjects of Great Britain, particularly in the respect to Morals and on the means of improving it."
1792	Grant finishes his first draft of the treatise, in which he states his belief that India is a state that suffers from depravity. He further suggests that the remedy to the apparent depravity is the "healing principle," namely, the supersession of the religions in India by Christianity through the diffusion of European science and literature. He propagates that in order to disseminate this knowledge, Persian should be replaced by the English language as both the official language and the language of instruction in education.
1800	Fort William College is set up in Calcutta by Governor-General Lord Wellesley as an academy of Oriental studies aimed at training British officials in the languages of the subcontinent.
1813	The Charter of the East India Company is renewed for another 20 years. Under Clause 43, a sum of not less than one lakh rupees per annum is set aside for "the revival and improvement of literature, and for the encouragement of the learned natives of India, and for the introduction and promotion of knowledge of sciences among the inhabitants of the British territories in India."[10] At this point in time, "literature" is largely assumed to be Indian literature and "encouragement of the learned natives" is construed as a provision of support to scholars studying in Oriental colleges.
1817	James Mill, a believer of the utilitarian principle and chief ally of Jeremy Bentham, publishes *The History of British India*. This magnum opus, which took 12 years to write, critiques the backward culture and customs of India, including *suttee*.[11] Mill promotes the introduction of western science and knowledge as a solution to India's apparent stagnancy.
1819	James Mill is appointed to a place in the India House as assistant to the examiner of India correspondence
1823	The General Committee of Public Instruction – which looked after education in Calcutta, the headquarters of the company in India – is established.
1823-1824	Members with Orientalist attitudes towards the language debate dominate the Committee of Public Instruction. They support native literature and classical education, and they argue against the imposition of the English language on native Indian people. They maintain that their actions are within the ambit of the Charter Act of 1813, and that their policies would change only if the Act is amended by the Parliament.
1823 (April)	James Mill is promoted to Assistant Examiner of Indian Correspondence in the India House.
1823 (December)	Raja Ram Mohan Roy, founder of a socio-religious reform movement in India named Brahma Sabhaa, opposes the proposal made by the General Committee of Public Instruction to establish a Sanskrit College in Calcutta. Raja Ram Mohan Roy states that "the Sanskrit system of education would be best calculated to keep this country in darkness if such has been the policy of British legislature."[12] However, the Committee continues to remain indifferent, and Oriental colleges are established in Calcutta, Delhi and Agra simultaneously. The Orientalists plead their case as "the metaphysical sciences, as found in Sanskrit and Arabic writing are, we believe, fully as worthy of being studied in those languages as in any other."[13]

(*Continued*)

Table 2.1 (Continued)

1824 (February)	The Court of Directors of the Company send a strongly worded despatch, bearing James Mill's stamp, condemning the work of the General Committee of Public Instruction. They call the work "fundamentally erroneous" and reiterate to the committee that "the great end should not have been to teach Hindu learning or Muhamedan learning, but useful learning."[14]
1827	William Bentinck is nominated as the Governor-General of the East India Company's possessions in India.
1828	Bentinck arrives in India as the Governor-General.
1828	Opinions on the nature of the company's policies towards the education of the people of India are polarised. On one hand, some Indians like Raja Ram Mohan Roy, as well as some British officials back home, like James Mill, are inclined towards English as the mode of education. On the other hand, official position of the company in India, dictated by the General Committee of Public Instruction, is dominated by persons with great admiration for Sanskrit and Arabic literature. The committee therefore uses the money allocated under Clause 43 of the Charters Act of 1813 to revive Indian literature.
1834 (June)	Thomas Macaulay arrives in India as the Law-Member of the Governor-General's Council.
1834 (December)	Macaulay is also appointed as the President of the General Committee of Public Instruction by Governor-General Bentinck, for his known intelligence and intellectual attainments.
	At this time, Bentinck asks Macaulay to provide his views on the subject of English education in India.
1835 (2 February)	Macaulay records a long rhetorical report promoting strongly a case for the introduction of the English language in India as a medium to disseminate scientific knowledge. He holds out a threat to resign if his recommendation is not accepted.[15]
1835 (7 March)	Bentinck issues the following order:
	"His Lordship-in-Council is of the opinion that the great object of the British Government ought to be the promotion of European literature and science among the natives of India, and that all funds appropriated for the purpose of education would be best employed on English education alone.
	His Lordship-in-Council directs that all the funds which these reforms will leave at the disposal of the Committee be henceforth employed in imparting to the Native population knowledge of English literature and science through the medium of the English language."[16]

Source: Compiled by author.

Charles Grant

The will of the East India Company to introduce the English language in India can be traced as far back as 1767, when an official named Charles Grant arrived in India. Grant has been historically famous for championing social reforms driven by his evangelical Christianity, particularly in India. However, his role in the story of the introduction of the English Language in India, though a subset of his famous social reform propagations, was explicitly brought into the historical narrative by Suresh Chandra Ghosh in 1995.

After his arrival in India as a company official, Grant attained a great fortune due to the loot and plunder that followed the Battles of Plassey and Buxar. With access to these riches, he led a spendthrift life in the country till 1786, after which a great change came over him due to the death of his younger brother and two little daughters in a short span of time.[17] He considered these family mishaps as "divine punishment for his ungodly past"[18] and thereafter, decided to live as a sincere and devout Christian who made evangelisation of India his divine mission.

It is famously believed that this introspective revelation led Grant to return to England in 1790 and start writing his treatise titled *Observations on the state of society among the Asiatic subjects of Great Britain, particularly in the respect to Morals and on the means of improving it.* This treatise – the draft of which was completed by 1792 – served as the first of many opinions that criticised native India of depravity and debasement. Grant attributed corruption and dishonesty to the Hindus, and he stated that along with fraudulence, the Hindus were also believers of barbaric customs like *suttee*. He further attributed to the Muslims debauchery and lawlessness, and he propagated that the interaction between the Hindus and Muslims had further debased them. Given his negative opinion of the Hindu and Muslim creeds, Grant argued that the company should remedy the situation rather than be apathetic. His proposed remedy, termed as the "healing principle," encompassed the supersession of the existing Indian religions by Christianity through the diffusion of western knowledge. He believed that only Christianity and western knowledge could enlighten the Indians out of their degeneracy and into "a world of new ideas."[19] Prophetically, Grant recommended that the most feasible way to disseminate this knowledge, which was captured in European literature and science, would be through the medium of the English language, since translating the existing knowledge into the Indian languages would not be efficacious.

Grant's suggested approach for introducing Christianity and western knowledge in India through the medium of the English language included three broad steps, encompassing first, replacement of Persian by English as the official language so as to induce the Indians to learn English; second, introduction of English as the medium of instruction and education, and avoidance of translation of European literatures and science into Indian languages in order to be more efficacious; and third, dissemination and disbursement of European education to the masses by young Indians trained in English.

Grant's observations, which he published as a book in 1797 in London, thus became the first published work to use the rationale of educating the apparently debased and immoral masses of India to promote the introduction of the English language in the country.

James Mill

While Charles Grant's role in the origin of the English language in India is undermined in common wisdom, James Mill's role is completely overlooked. This omission is not surprising, given that Mill, though highly regarded in his day, is now primarily remembered for being an ally of Jeremy Bentham and the father of John Stuart Mill. His contribution as a political philosopher, historian, economist, educational theorist and legal reformer, is often overshadowed by his relationship with the aforementioned eminent figures. Particularly, with regards to the English language in India, Mill's role is unheeded because he never explicitly propagated the implementation of the western language in the Indian social and educational infrastructure.

Yet, as Donald Winch rightly states, no volume of James Mill would be complete if it did not take into account his role in the Indian affairs,[20] and, by extension, the historical narrative of Indian affairs would be incomplete if it did not consider James Mill's role in it. Ironically, his most important contribution to the language domain in the Indian context stemmed from his writings on secondary literature, without any primary visit to India. This *magnum opus*, titled *The History of British India*, took 12 years to write and was published in 1817. What should have been an apology for writing a narrative on India without ever having visited the country or being aware of the indigenous languages, was actually portrayed as a qualification by Mill who stated that

> whatever is worth seeing or hearing in India, can be expressed in writing. As soon as everything of importance is expressed in writing, a man who is duly qualified may obtain more knowledge of India in one year in his closet in England, than he could obtain during the course of the longest life, by the use of his eyes and his ears in India.[21]

He argued that his ignorance of India and its languages enabled him to understand the country's culture comprehensively and objectively from a distance through translated versions of its literature.

Published 25 years after Grant made his observations, Mill's *History* contained similar reformist arguments critical of existing Indian culture and literature, after an apparent objective perusal. He described Indian historical records and literature as the "offspring of a rude and ungoverned imagination," stating that the Indian culture was based on imagination-driven literature, including such epics as the *Bhagavad Gita* and the *Ramayana*.[22] Opposing this construction of culture on a foundation of imagination, and adhering to David Hartley's associationist psychology (which propagated the association of ideas as the mind's organising principle), Mill provided the evidence of his problem with Indian literature and culture.

Additionally, Mill criticised the form of government in India, in which the

> sovereign governed by a sort of council, composed of Brahmens, who exercised the powers of government, according to no pre-established plan; but according as each by intrigue, or by reputation, could obtain an ascendancy among the rest.[23]

The oriental despotism that existed in India under Hindu and Mahomedan rulers, worsened by the power transfer by the sovereign into the hands of the priests (more so in the Hindu system of government), went against Mill's utilitarian philosophy, which was very much a secular one.[24] *The History of British India*, as Yale's Associate Professor of Political Science, Karuna Mantena, rightly puts it, was thus a "full-scale assault" on any claimed achievements of Indian literature and government.[25]

Mill proposed the rejection of the Indian society, deeming it corrupt, and claimed it to be a hostile condition to base ideal governmental institutions. Suggesting that the superstitious and apathetic characteristics of the Indian subjects was a function of religious tyranny and governmental despotism, he proposed the need for liberal political and legal reforms propagated by western knowledge.

This monumental book is of relevance to the narrative of the English language in India for two reasons. First, though it did not provide the same conclusion, it echoed Charles Grant's observations' premise. It spoke of the prevalence of a set of initial conditions encompassing a decadent and debased society in dire need of western knowledge and intervention, which made India a hotbed for English language implementation. Second, its popularity paved the way for Mill's appointment to the East India Company in 1819, thereby giving him the position to convert his theory into practice. And convert he did, as evidenced by the fact that when the General Committee of Public Instruction in India (responsible for the education in Calcutta, the headquarters of the company) was dominated by officials of orientalist inclination in 1824, the Court of Directors of the company sent a strongly worded despatch bearing James Mill's stamp. This despatch condemned the work of the General Committee of Public Instruction as "fundamentally erroneous" and stated that "the great end should not have been to teach Hindu learning or Muhamedan learning, but useful learning."[26]

Thus, similar to Grant, Mill's role encompassed the provision of the theoretical underpinning for western knowledge, and by extension, western language, as he became an important intellectual influence in shaping Indian policies. His role in the language narrative got further extended by the clout he garnered as an official of Indian correspondence of the company, through which he influenced the very body responsible for education in British India.

Thomas Babington Macaulay

At the time when James Mill was writing his monumental critique of Indian society in 1813, the Charter of the East India Company was renewed for another 20 years, and a sum of not less than one lakh rupees per annum was set aside under Clause 43 for "the revival and improvement of literature, and for the encouragement of the learned natives of India, and for the introduction and promotion of knowledge of sciences among the inhabitants of the British territories in India."[27] What is significant is that at that time no specification was made regarding the language that would be used to spread this education in India. Since that was left ambiguous, it was assumed that education would be conducted and enriched through Indian literature. As stated previously, the General Committee of Public Instruction, which acted in strict interpretation of Clause 43 of the Charter Act of 1813, had an orientalist inclination at the time, as it was dominated by persons with great admiration for indigenous literature. Therefore, the committee spent the said amount on the revival of oriental learning and institutions as well as on the encouragement of learned Indians.

Though Mill's despatch of 1824 condemned this stance of the committee, the situation remained largely orientalist in practice up until 2 February 1835, when Thomas Babington Macaulay delivered his famous "Minutes." Through his long rhetorical report, Macaulay propagated his belief that the "revival and improvement of literature," which was largely assumed to be Indian literature, was incoherent with the "promotion of knowledge of sciences," as no one could achieve the latter without understanding the language in which the "poetry of Milton, the metaphysics of Locke, and the physics of Newton"[28] was written. If scientific knowledge was to be introduced and enriched amongst the inhabitants of British India, the English language was a mandatory requirement. History credits this delivery as the immediate reason for the implementation of the English language in India.

Macaulay became a member of the British Parliament in 1830, kicking off his tenure with a maiden speech propagating the abolishment of civil disabilities of Jews in Britain. Since his inception as a politician, he propagated liberal and progressive, yet nonetheless imperialist, ideologies. These beliefs extended to the Indian domain, which he entered with the passing of the Government of India Act in 1833 as the Secretary of the Board of

Control under Lord Grey. Through this Act, William Bentinck became the first Governor-General of India, and Macaulay became his advisor as the Law-Member of the Governor-General's Council from 1834. As advisor, Macaulay spoke extensively of the depravity and debasement that existed in India, with a clear recommendation – spread European knowledge in the subcontinent through the dissemination of the English language.

It is evident that Macaulay echoed the premise laid out by Mill in 1817 and Grant in 1790. The coherence between Macaulay's minutes and Mill's critique – pertaining to Indian knowledge's imaginative base – is substantiated by the former's statement: "when we pass from works of *imagination* to works in which facts are recorded and general principles investigated, the superiority of the Europeans becomes absolutely immeasurable." His shared opinion with Grant, pertaining to the debasement of native India, existed even before he came to India, and it is substantiated by the speech that he gave to the British Parliament on 10 July 1833, one year before his arrival into India as the Law-Member of the Governor-General's Council:

> It is scarcely possible to calculate the benefits which we might derive from the diffusion of European civilisation among the vast population of the East. What is power worth if it is founded on vice, on ignorance, and on misery; if we can hold it only by violating the most sacred duties which as governors we owe to the governed, and which, as a people blessed with a far more than ordinary measure of political liberty and of intellectual light, we owe to a race debased by three thousand years of despotism and priest craft?[29]

Through this speech, Macaulay, prior to arriving in India, had credited to British imperialism the attributes of altruism, and cultural and intellectual supremacy. These accreditations were in line with those presented by Mill and Grant.

Additionally, Macaulay's recommendation for the apparent decadence of the East – through diffusion of European knowledge using the medium of the English language – ricocheted and replicated those proposed by Grant 43 years prior. According to Ghosh, there were four main themes of Macaulay's report: first, English should replace Persian as the official language; second, English should be introduced as the medium of instruction in all the education institutions as "(the) language has ready access to all the vast intellectual wealth which all the wisest nations of the earth have created and hoarded in the course of ninety generations"; third, Indians well acquainted with western knowledge and science would enrich and help "raise up a good vernacular literature in the country" within 20 years due to their "inclination and the ability to exhibit European knowledge in the vernacular dialects"; and fourth, Indians taught through the medium of English would take care of the education of their own countrymen.[30]

Scholars believe that the works of Mill and Grant influenced these clear English language-promoting themes. While Mill's *The History of British India* was often referred to when discussing the company's affairs in India in the mid-1800s, Grant's treatise was reprinted as a House of Commons document in 1813 and 1833. It wouldn't be unreasonable to believe that both of these works were contemporarily accessible to the erudite Macaulay. Nonetheless, while the propagation of western language gained its initial thrust during the utilitarian years, with Grant providing the preliminary theoretical justification, Macaulay's recommendation remains the immediate factor leading to the implementation of the English language in India given his political positioning. Macaulay acted upon his will to "civilise" Indian society by diffusing European science and knowledge, and the English language became the medium to achieve this end, as he observed that "the languages of Western Europe civilised Russia. I cannot doubt that they will do for the Hindoo what they have done for the tartar."

Overall, Macaulay's recommendation provided a crucial thrust in the English implementation process in India. The report created a sensational stir from its inception, and within four years, large parts of the report were made public by the efforts of Charles Edward Trevelyan (who was also Macaulay's brother-in-law). Within 100 years, it had been partially or fully published on nine different occasions.[31] His role in the narrative being so powerfully defined that his name became a noun – "Macaulayism" – to refer to policies or acts that eliminate indigenous cultures through westernisation of the education system.

William Bentinck

The consequence of Macaulay's recommendation was the acceptance by the then Governor General William Bentinck, on 7 March 1835, that "the great object of the British Government ought to be the promotion of European literature and science among Indians."[32] This acceptance was closely followed by the necessary order given by Bentinck to reorganise funds for "imparting to the native population a knowledge of English literature and science through the medium of the English language."[33] While many limit Bentinck's role in the historical account as simply passing an order whose foundation was set by Macaulay, some scholars disagree with this circumscription. Scholars such as Percival Spear (1938), Kenneth Ballhatchet (1951) and Suresh Chandra Ghosh (1995), believe that Bentinck's role in the introduction of the language in India is highly undermined in the past literature on the subject, and they highlight that Bentinck's inclination towards the dissemination of the English language and education in India existed long before Macaulay's recommendation. In this aspect, Macaulay's "Minute on Indian Education" was simply a catalyst and was not a decisive influence, as substantiated by the writing of Spear:

> For this to have been the case, it must be assumed that without his (Macaulay's) intervention the result might have been otherwise. Macaulay has been too much praised and too much blamed; his contribution was like the lightning flash which vividly illumines the storm and reveals the landscape, albeit in fantastic proportions and bewildering lights, but which neither directs its course nor ordains its conclusion.[34]

These scholars push Macaulay's report into the background and instead argue that Bentinck had already effectively made his Anglicist decision before Macaulay even arrived. In this context, Macaulay simply provided a theoretical underpinning to Bentinck's beliefs and gave him the necessary thrust to pursue practical action on the subject.

Ghosh justifies this by providing a detailed history of Bentinck's role in the dissemination of the English language in India. The author notes that Bentinck was nominated as the Governor-General of the East India Company's possessions in India in December 1827. By the time Bentinck arrived in India in July 1828, there already existed an immense interest to learn English amongst the Indians in the metropolitan cities of British India. While some enlightened Indians like Raja Ram Mohan Roy saw the English language, and the resultant European knowledge, as a means to end the dogmatism and vicious superstitions that existed in the country, other young Indians saw it as a medium to increase their employment opportunities in various British establishments. As mentioned previously, at this time, contrary to the changing domestic trends and interests, the General Committee of Public Instruction continued to display oriental inclinations. Nonetheless, the growing local interest among young Indians to learn English was coherent with the utilitarian force emerging in England – a renowned propagator of which was none other than James Mill. Bentinck was a firm believer of utilitarianism and an ardent follower of James Mill. What substantiates Bentinck's inclination towards Mill and utilitarianism, and thus by extension his inclination towards the introduction of western knowledge in India, are his words to Mill during his farewell dinner on the eve of his departure to India: "I am going to British India but I shall not be the Governor-General. It is you that will be the Governor-General."[35]

This evident utilitarian influence on Bentinck suggests that he had been "steadily pursuing a policy of gradual introduction of English education in India since 1829."[36] His superior positioning in India gave him the required authority to mobilise and implement the utilitarian principles in the seemingly dogmatic country. For instance, he abolished *suttee* and took measures to suppress *thugee*[37] and curb infanticide. Since Bentinck had this history of condemning and attacking what he saw as barbaric practices, it seems evident, Ghosh argues, that he would have formed his own Anglicist opinions about education – which was the much-propagated remedy of barbarism. And indeed, Bentinck did, substantiating the idea in his letter to Mancy on 1 June 1834:

> General education is my panacea for the regeneration of India. The ground must be prepared and the jungle cleared away before the human mind can receive, with any prospect of real benefit, the seeds of improvement You will anticipate my entire dissent from those who think it better that the natives should remain in ignorance. I cannot regard the advantage of ignorance to the governors or the governed. If our rule is bad, as I believe it to be, let the natives have the means, through knowledge, to represent their grievances and to obtain redress. If their own habits, morals or way of thinking are inconsistent with their own happiness and improvement, let them have the means provided by our greater intelligence of discovering their errors. **I approve therefore of every plan by which the human mind can be instructed and of course elevated.**"[38]

The referred "*plan*" to "*elevate*" was none other than the dissemination of western knowledge through the implementation of the English language as the medium of instruction, and of this Bentinck was certain as early as 1829. Why else would he write to Charles Metcalfe (who would subsequently succeed him as the Governor-General) in September 1829 a letter stating that "the British language" was "the key of all improvements?"[39]

What further reiterates the notion that Bentinck's role superseded that of Macaulay's in the historical account, beyond his spoken and written words, are the actions that he took prior to Macaulay's report. These actions encompassed the gradual replacement of Persian by English in all official works, accompanied by the spread the English language in all education institutions. For instance, he influenced young Indians to learn English by opening up subordinate positions in judicial and revenue branches to English educated Indians. Additionally, he urged the General Committee of Public Instruction to recognise the importance of English by stating, in a letter on 26 June 1929, that

> It is the wish and admitted policy of the British Government to render its own language gradually and eventually the language of public business throughout the country, and that it will omit no opportunity of giving every reasonable and practical degree of encouragement to the execution of this project.[40]

Out of respect for the wishes of the Governor-General, the General Committee of Public Instruction added English classes to the Benares Sanskrit College curriculum in 1830, thereby providing English classes in all the important oriental institutions in Calcutta, Delhi and Benares. Moreover, he extended his support to missionaries that used English as the medium of instruction in their educational institutions, including the Scottish missionary Alexander Duff, who set up the General Assembly's Institution in Calcutta in 1830.

Nonetheless, the most influential thrust to Bentinck's "plan" for elevation came from Macaulay's report on 2 February 1835 as expert advice on the subject, and Bentinck immediately acted on it. Ghosh highlights a very interesting point – according to norms of the East India Company, the Governor-General was not permitted to initiate any important action without first getting the approval of the Court of Directors in London. Furthermore, in those days of steamship navigation, a despatch from Calcutta took no less than three months to reach London. Since Bentinck acted on Macaulay's recommendation within a few weeks, Ghosh states that Bentinck did not obtain the required sanction from the Court of Directors. This simple fact proves that Bentinck acted without the permission of the East India Company. While Arthur Mayhew argues that Bentinck took this decision even without reading Macaulay's reports and acted solely because of Macaulay's threat to resign,[41] Ghosh, Spear and Ballhatchet attribute this hurried approval to Bentinck's own desire to implement the western language in India. It is believed that Bentinck was considering retiring by March 1835, and ergo, wanted to introduce the English language in India speedily. The disregard for the required consent was so as to avoid leaving the fate of a subject so imperative to him at the hands of a successor. Thus, he passed the order on 7 March 1935 that changed the fate of millions – the Indians of that period, the Indian in the generations to come and Bentinck himself. While he was compelled to withdraw the company's affairs from the Court of Directors, the destiny of India changed.

So what was the reason?

Evidently, the implementation of the English language in India was an area passionately pursued by many officials of the company. While some theoretically made a case for the language and pursued practical actions, others provided their support for pro-English initiatives. The axiomatic question that arises is why was English language implementation an agenda for the company in India? Generally, the agreed upon answer is twofold.

The first reasoning was the one explicitly stated by the company as the official justification for the introduction of the western language. This reasoning entailed that the Indian society was decadent with barbaric rituals and dogmatic superstitions, and the only remedy for such debauchery was the inculcation of knowledge. Only scientific knowledge could cure a "race debased by three thousand years of despotism and priest-craft,"[42] and the English language was the necessary medium for the dissemination of the said cure in India.

However, many scholars, including Badri Raina, suggest that there existed a second implicit reason, which Britain covered under the pretext of knowledge dissemination to further their agenda.[43] These scholars maintain the belief that the establishment of English was for the sole purpose of serving the end of British administration in India, as the company wanted to create a tier of clerks who would fill the lower ranks. In this context, the introduction of English had less to do with "improvement of literature" and "promotion of knowledge," and more to do with building a tier of English-speaking Indians subservient to the British. This notion is substantiated by Macaulay's testimony that

> (the British) must at present do our best to form a class who may be interpreters between us and the millions whom we govern – a class of persons Indian in blood and colour, but English in tastes, in opinion, in morals and in intellect.[44]

Given the two reasons, English establishment in India had two clear telos from the outset – one paternalistic and the other colonial. It was to spread knowledge, but this knowledge was to be constricted to the upper and middle classes of urban society. This constriction, which led to the creation of a tier of Indian *babus* during the British *Raj*, has today perpetuated into the creation of the present day Indian elites.

Overall, the introduction of the English language in India was a result of Britain's imperialist conquest of the country, and it was implemented for the purpose of a) imparting western knowledge amongst the native Indians and b) creating a tier of anglicised elite Indians. The next section of this book will highlight how these two purposes prevailed, even after Britain's exit from India, and how they became prominent reasons for the prevalence of the language in independent India.

The legacy

> *Why a language becomes a global language has little to do with the number of people who speak it. It is much more to do with who those speakers are.*
>
> – (David Crystal, 2003)

The British left India in 1947 after huge waves of nationalism. Despite the exit of the native speakers, the English language sustained and was proclaimed the associate official language of the Union Government. It wouldn't be erroneous to state that the extension of the two reasons that justified the *introduction* of the language, became the reasons for its *prevalence* post-independence.

First, Britain's justification of creating a tier of elite Indians with an anglicised education paved the way for the anglicised and elite identities of freedom fighters responsible for the independence movement. The identities of these persons became the immediate cause for the English language legacy post-independence. Second, Britain's justification of imparting western knowledge to the natives paved the way for an Indian education and administration system greatly interwoven with the English language. This dependence of educational and political institutions of the multilingual India on English became the subsequent cause of the language's retention.

Immediate legacy: the identities of the persons responsible for the independence movement

Bentinck's order paved the way for the ensuing segregation of Indians into two categories on linguistic bases – the English-educated Indian *babus* and the remaining Indian masses. The core group of freedom fighters, attributed with the achievement of gaining independence for India, consisted of these Indian *babus* who conversed in English. Since a language's dominance in a region is dependent on the identities of the speakers rather than the number of speakers, the reason for the persistence of the English language in India post-independence can be ascribed to the fact that the people responsible for India's freedom were English speakers cultivated in an anglicised system of education.

Even though they were given a relatively superior status in the Indian society, these *babus* had more reasons to seek freedom. This was prophesised as early as 1884 by the then-Viceroy, Lord Ripon, who wrote to the then-Secretary of State for India, Lord Kimberley, stating that

> you may rely upon it that there are few Indian questions of greater importance in the present day than those which relate to the mode in which we are to deal with the growing body of natives educated by ourselves in Western learning and Western ideas.[45]

Having received an anglicised education through the English medium, the *babus* were shadows of the British as Macaulay had envisaged. Nonetheless, they were nowhere close to reaching and achieving the superiority that Britain had reserved for its own members, and this became a reason for their displeasure and provocation. For instance, many educated Indians wished for employment in the East India Company only to fail, substantiating which is the whopping figure in 1857 of 500 graduates who had desired to join the company in Bengal alone.

Additionally, they found it almost impossible to obtain positions in the Indian administration commensurate with their education and qualifications. Though the 1853 Charter Act theoretically opened up the covenanted

Indian Civil Service, the cream of the Indian administration, to all Indian subjects between the ages of 18 and 23, entry was through a competitive examination that was to be held in England only. Hopeful Indian candidates, who were already drenched in the financial and social pressures of travelling abroad for the examination, were further handicapped when the upper age limit was reduced from 23 in 1853 to 19 by 1876. Convinced, in the words of one Viceroy, of the "essential and insurmountable distinctions of race qualities," most British officials did not regard the educated Indian *babus* as suitable material for the more senior positions within the civil service. Therefore, when Satyendra Nath Tagore in 1863 became the first Indian to pass the entrance examination due to his exceptionally high marks in Arabic and Sanskrit, the concerned authorities in England reduced the marks allocated to these subjects and cancelled a scholarship scheme that had been designed to enable nine Indian students to travel to England each year for higher education.[46]

By 1887, approximately 12 Indians had entered the covenanted service through open competition. With so few gaining admission, the majority of English-educated Indian *babus* turned instead to law and teaching, politics and journalism, or a combination of both. These figures included: Man Mohan Ghose, the first Indian barrister who read for the London bar after two failures in the civil service examination in 1864 and 1865; Woomesh Chandra Bonnerjee, the first president of the Indian National Congress in 1885; Dadabhai Naoroji, the figure instrumental in establishing the London India Society in 1865 and the East India Association in 1866 (both the organisations were created to influence British opinion on Indian questions); and many more. Mohandas Karamchand Gandhi, the Father of independent India and the key independence figure, was an English-speaking Indian who was aggravated by British discrimination. Evidently, the major players of the Indian National Congress, formulated in 1885, were the English-educated *babus* who went ahead to form the first government of the independent India.

Given this backdrop, it is reasonable to construe that though the British provided a tier of Indians with the opportunity to learn the English language and the associated anglicised education, they still circumscribed their opportunities in terms of employment, thereby providing them with not only a reason to retaliate but also the skills to do so effectively. Since an independent India was a consequence of the work of these English-speaking *babus*, the legacy of the English language prevailed after the British exit.

Subsequent legacy: education and administration of multilingual India

At the time of independence, there was great discourse on the topic of the official language of India and the status of English as the medium of instruction in educational institutions, both schools and colleges. While some patriots wanted to rid India of the colonial language and instead adopt an indigenous Indian one as the national language, others believed that the infrastructure of Indian administration and education had become so largely and intrinsically dependent on English during the British reign that it would simply be infeasible to instantaneously do away with the language. Thanks to Britain's rationalisation of disseminating knowledge throughout native India to introduce English, the language had become a dominant part of the education and political institutions of twentieth-century India. After all, it had played a key role in these areas since the past 112 years. The anti-Hindi agitations in the southern state of Tamil Nadu in 1948–1950, opposing the implementation of Hindi as a compulsory language in schools, further tilted the balance towards the retention of English. The Union government realised this dependence of the Indian administration and education system on the language and thereby declared through the constitution of India in 1950 that "for a period of fifteen years from the commencement of the constitution, English language shall continue to be used for all the official purposes of the Union for which it was being used immediately before such commencement."[47]

In terms of education, attempts were made to analyse the situation in order to reduce India's dependence on English. The first education commission of independent India, which was a University Education Commission named the Radhakrishnan Commission (1948), provided support for a shift from English to Indian languages as a medium for instruction in higher education. The commission proposed a three-language approach for students at higher secondary and university stages – the regional language, the federal language and English. Understanding the importance of English in Indian academic life, the commission propagated that, along with Indian languages, English should also be studied so that India can "keep in touch with the living stream of ever growing knowledge." Thus, though the commission recommended the learning of English, it simultaneously propagated a restrictive use through promotion of Hindi and regional languages.

The Secondary Education Review, established in 1951–1952, reviewed the position of the English language again, only to further extend support for the western language. The commission reiterated the recommendation of the Radhakrishna Commission and stated that:

> "no student should be handicapped by the ignorance of a language which will ultimately determine the career that he should choose. It should also be recognized that even in regard to many of the diversified courses of instruction, as matters stand at present, a full knowledge of English will be extremely useful for further study of the same subject. All those considerations lead to the conclusion that English should be given due position in secondary schools."[48]

This commission laid emphasis on retaining a regional language or mother tongue as the medium of instruction at the secondary stage of education and promoted the teaching of English as a separate subject, thereby propagating a two-language formula. However, by 1956, the Central Advisory Board of Education reversed back to a three-language approach due to the difficulties faced by the non-Hindi speaking population. This approach garnered further support during the Conference of Chief Ministers in 1961. Evidently, the use of a single indigenous Indian language as the sole medium of education was proving to be extremely difficult in practice given the linguistic diversity, thereby making the process of replacement of English within 15 years, as stated in the Constitution, a difficult goal to attain.

In 1955, the University Grants Commission set up a committee headed by Dr H.N. Kunzru to look specifically at the problem of the medium of education. The committee noted two prominent deterrents of reverting from English: first, translation of books, especially those used for higher education, into regional languages required Herculean efforts; and second, the university teachers refused to teach in any language other than English since they themselves had been trained in it. Given these practical and reasonable hindrances, the committee concluded that change from English to an Indian language as a medium of instruction at the university level cannot and should not be hurried. It further suggested that even when the right time comes for the shift to be made, adequate knowledge of English as a second language should still be given to the students, as that would be in India's educational interest. Consistent with this, the Official Language Commission (1956) made the recommendation that English must be retained as the medium for competitive examinations for All India Services until the time non-Hindi speaking candidates can compete with Hindi speakers on equal terms by learning Hindi as the medium, or alternatively until all major regional languages can be made mediums for these competitive examinations.

With all these pro-English recommendations, the government of the time had to accept that hastily removing the English language from the education sector was not a feasible option due to three major reasons. First, at the university level, teachers themselves were trained in English and were therefore inclined towards English medium higher education. To enable students to have a smooth higher education experience, a proper foundation in English had to be laid at the secondary school level, thereby making the English language essential even in schools. Second, training the linguistically diverse pupils of India to learn the indigenous language, Hindi, as the medium of education was proving to be extremely difficult. The non-Hindi speaking South and North East were relatively more comfortable with and skilled in English and axiomatically favoured it over Hindi. This discomfort ultimately manifested in various riots, demonstrations and violence. During an All India Language Conference in 1958, attended by representatives of Tamil, Malayalam, Telugu, Oriya, Marathi, Assamese, Bengali and

Kannada languages, it was declared that "Hindi is as foreign to non-Hindi speaking people as English is to the protagonists of Hindi."[49] Third, English was still the most efficacious medium to obtain scientific and western knowledge, given that the regional languages of India had not yet developed to a point where they could replace English. Furthermore, even if these regional languages became sufficiently developed, translation of books into these varying languages would be a herculean task.

Evidently, the heterogeneity of India was making it difficult to narrow down to one indigenous language. While Hindi was being opposed by non-Hindi speakers, other regional languages did not have a sufficient number of native speakers and/or were not sufficiently developed to be the medium of instruction. The consequence of these problems was the realisation by the then-Home Minister of India, Lal Bahadur Shastri, that "a sudden change without the boys and girls learning one of the official languages could result in the compartmentalisation of the country, which India could not afford. English has to remain a compulsory language for some time to come."[50] The realisation was further strengthened by the introduction of the Official Language Bill of 1963, supported by the then Prime Minister, Jawaharlal Nehru, which proposed a removal of the restriction placed by the Constitution of India on the use of English beyond 1965. Leading members of the anti-Hindi camp, such as Annadurai, propagated an *indefinite* continuation of the status quo of English as an associate official language, as that would "distribute advantages and disadvantages evenly" amongst Hindi and non-Hindi speakers of India.[51]

However, the death of Jawaharlal Nehru in 1964 increased apprehension amongst the anti-Hindi camp that his assurance of 1963 would not be kept. Efforts made by some ministries and departments of the Government of India to switch from English to Hindi further embedded these apprehensions. For instance, the Home Ministry and the Information and Broadcasting Ministry, headed by Gulzarilal Nanda and Indira Gandhi respectively, issued circulars for replacing English with Hindi from 26 January 1965 – the date that marked the end of the 15-year retention period of English proposed by the Constitution of 1950. The unfortunate consequence of such government measures was a violent language agitation, especially in the southern state of Madras (Chennai) in Tamil Nadu, in 1965. Several agitators committed suicide by self-immolation and consumption of poison, with the death toll reaching an official figure of 70.

The impact of the agitation was a radio broadcast made on 11 February 1966 by the then Prime Minister, Lal Bahadur Shastri, that he would honour Nehru's assurance – English would continue to be used for central and interstate communication and All India Civil Services examinations would continue to be conducted in English. What followed was an amendment in 1967 to modify the 1963 Bill to guarantee "virtual indefinite policy of bilingualism,"[52] i.e. Hindi and English, in official transactions.

The Parliament thereafter passed the Official Languages Act along with the amendment. This amended act completely reversed the goals of the official language policy from promoting an indigenous language within a period, and instead promoted the status of English to a higher position vis-à-vis Hindi and other regional languages.

Thereafter, more agitations resisting Hindi further strengthened the English language's hold on the education and governance of India. For instance, the 1968 student agitation in Tamil Nadu removed the three-language education approach in the state by eliminating Hindi from the curriculum. It further urged the central government to halt the special status attributed to Hindi in the Constitution and treat all regional languages equally. Such acts further reiterated the relevance and embedded the grasp of the English language in India by assuring that no single indigenous language could gain a national status.

Indigenous reasons for retention post-independence

Through this historical analysis of state of affairs in India post-independence, one can understand that Britain's rationalisation for introducing English got entrenched in the Indian system to such a degree that the newly independent state found it infeasible to eradicate the usage of the language. Britain's attempt to form a tier of anglicised Indians perpetuated into an army of elite Indians who were at the forefront of the independence movement. Its attempt to introduce western education in India resulted in an education system that was highly reliant on English as the medium to gain knowledge. However, there were two predominant indigenous factors, not created by the British, which further embedded the need for the English language in India – linguistic diversity and the anti-Hindi agitations.

The heterogeneity of India in terms of languages went a long way to ensure the persistence of the English language in the country even after the British exit. It became difficult to replace English with an indigenous language given the sheer number of options available. A quantification of this theoretical link between heterogeneity of languages and dependence on English in the Indian context can be extrapolated from the 2011 paper by scholars Mehtabul Azam, Aimee Chin and Nishith Prakash. In "The Returns to English-Language Skills in India," the scholars stated that as of 2005, English-speaking ability was higher in those districts of India that had greater linguistic diversity in 1961.[53]

It is noteworthy that in term of numbers, Hindi speakers greatly outnumbered English speakers, yet mass agitations were against Hindi. It might be incorrect to state that these riots and demonstrations in South India were pro-English, yet the solution of retaining English did appease the situation. Thus, one can construe that though the number of Hindi speakers were greater in India, they were geographically concentrated to the North. On the other hand, while English speakers were relatively less in number, their geographical placement was dispersed throughout India – North, South, East and West – thereby giving English an edge over Hindi as an appeaser of linguistic sentiments.

In summation, the legacy of this foreign language remained in the country even after its native speakers left due to the administrative ease it bought to the newly sovereign heterogeneous nation, the constitution of which was established by an army of English-speaking *babus*.

The current picture

> *Once when I was interviewing perhaps the most famous son of the Doon school, Rajiv Gandhi, I said in Hindi "Put the microphone a little lower." When he heard this, Rajiv Gandhi said to me "You speak very good Hindi." I said "I wish I spoke it better." He laughed, and said "I wish I did, too."*
>
> – (Mark Tully, 1996)

One would have assumed that the elitism and popularity associated with the English language would subsequently disappear as years went by, and India got time to replace the British legacies they were compelled to adopt at the initial stages of independence for administrative stability. Indeed, India made efforts to free itself of these legacies as much as it could, substantiating the various states, streets and institutions it renamed over the years. Alas, if only substituting a language was as simple as substituting a name! Not only did the English language dodge constituting as rehabilitated legacy, it also ensured that it maintained the surfeit esteem it held 72 years back.

An eminent reason for this persistent prevalence of the language stems from its dissemination into the economic arena. In contemporary India, the English language is no longer circumscribed as a provider of administrative and educational ease in a multilingual country. Today, the language is not only a medium of education and political administration, but it is also the medium of economic communication. In this regard, using the English language has become a necessary skill, thereby becoming a primary criterion for employment and increased wage returns in India. Let us look at a short analysis of the supply and demand of English speakers to better understand the dominance of the language in contemporary India.

Supply of English speakers

As per the 2011 Census data, a mere 259,678 Indians, approximating 0.02% of the country's population, reported English as their mother tongue. The 2001 Census had reported similar figures for nativity of speaking and had further suggested a 12% reportage of Indians who spoke English as their first, second or third language. A higher reported figure was provided by Mehtabul Azam, Aimee Chin and Nishith Prakash in their 2011 paper. Using the India Human Development Survey Round 1 data for 2005 (henceforth referred to as IHDS Round 1), which surveyed 41,554 households in 1503 villages and 971 urban neighbourhoods across India, the scholars tabulated the percentage of English speakers in India to be 20%. Of this, fluent English speakers constituted only 3.8%.[54]

To get the most recent tabulation of the supply of English speakers, I use the latest available data on English proficiency – India Human Development Survey Round 2 (henceforth, referred to as IHDS Round 2). Published in 2015, this dataset re-interviewed most of the 41,554 households of the Round 1 survey in 2011–2012. This survey, jointly organised by the National Council of Applied Economic Research (NCAER, New Delhi) and the University of Maryland, is the only nationally representative survey conducted in India that questions its interviewees about their English-speaking skills; it has a weighted sample of 729,428,794 individuals of working age population aged 18 to 65 (the non-weighted sample is 123,769).

An analysis of the latest data, with a comparison to the 2005 results presented by Mehtabul Azam, Aimee Chin and Nishith Prakash, is presented in Table 2.2. One must note however that the IHDS questionnaire asked the interviewees their own perception of whether they can speak English. Since the figures represent an individual's perception of their language proficiency rather than an objective tested representation, the figures provided might have an upwards bias. In that regards, it is reasonable to assume that the actual numbers of tested English speakers might indeed be lower.

As evident from the table, the latest figures reflect that 28.7% of India has English-speaking skills. 6.3% report themselves as fluent speakers, while 22.4% state that they have little English-speaking skills. The total number of English speakers in India has increased by 8.7% since 2005, with fluent speakers increasing by 2.5% and non-fluent speakers increasing by 6.2%.

Interestingly, each and every subpopulation category has witnessed an increasing number of English speakers relative to 2005. The only subcategory that shows a 6.4% reduction in the number of English speakers is the group with college, graduate or higher degrees who reported as having little English-speaking skills. However, within the same subpopulation, individuals who reported as having fluent English-speaking skills increased by 6.9%, thereby increasing the total number of English speakers in the category over the years.

Evidently, the number of English-speakers in India is on a continuous rise. Nevertheless, despite the gradual and consistent increase, 71.3% of the Indian population still has no English skills.

Table 2.2 Percentage of English speakers in India in 2005 and 2011[55]

	Percentage of Indians with Fluent English Ability (1)			*Percentage of Indians with Little English Ability (2)*			*Total Percentage of Indians with English Ability (3) = (1) + (2)*		
	2005	**2011**	**Change**	**2005**	**2011**	**Change**	**2005**	**2011**	**Change**
All Individual Aged 18–65	3.8	6.3	**+2.5**	16.2	22.4	**+6.2**	20.0	28.7	**+8.7**
By Gender									
Male	5.0	8.02	**+3.02**	21.0	27.0	**+6.0**	25.9	35.1	**+9.2**
Female	2.6	4.7	**+2.1**	11.5	17.9	**+6.4**	14.2	22.6	**+8.4**
By Age									
18–35	4.4	8.1	**+3.7**	20.2	28.3	**+8.1**	24.6	36.4	**+11.8**
36–50	3.3	4.5	**+1.2**	12.8	16.5	**+3.7**	16.1	21.0	**+4.9**
51–65	3.0	4.2	**+1.2**	9.7	14.4	**+4.7**	12.7	18.6	**+5.9**
By Educational Attainment									
No Completed Schooling	0.0	0.0	**0.0**	0.0	2.3	**+2.3**	0.0	2.3	**+2.3**
Some Primary (1–4 years of schooling)	0.1	0.2	**+0.1**	1.1	3.8	**+2.7**	1.2	4.0	**+2.8**
Primary (5–9)	0.5	0.9	**+0.4**	10.3	16.6	**+6.3**	10.8	17.5	**+6.7**
Secondary (10–14)	6.0	10.2	**+4.2**	49.5	52.8	**+3.3**	55.5	63.0	**+7.5**
College Graduate or Higher	35.3	42.2	**+6.9**	53.2	46.8	**- 6.4**	88.5	89.0	**+0.5**
By Social Group									
Scheduled Tribes	2.5	4.3	**+1.8**	8.4	15.5	**+7.1**	10.9	19.8	**+8.9**
Scheduled Caste	1.5	3.4	**+1.9**	11.4	17.8	**+6.4**	12.9	21.2	**+8.3**
Other Backward Castes	2.9	5.2	**+2.3**	14.7	21.9	**+7.2**	17.6	27.1	**+9.5**
General	7.6	10.7	**+3.1**	26.0	28.5	**+2.5**	33.6	39.2	**+5.6**
By Geography									
Urban	9.0	12.4	**+3.4**	25.8	30.2	**+4.4**	34.8	42.6	**+7.8**
Rural	1.7	3.2	**+1.5**	12.4	18.4	**+6.0**	14.1	21.6	**+7.5**

Source: The data for the year 2011 has been tabulated using the India Human Development Survey Round 2 published in 2015. The data for the year 2005 has been tabulated using the India Human Development Survey Round 1.

Demand for English speakers

Given the linguistic heterogeneity prominent in the country, the continuation of the usage of English language post-independence was surely a good interim solution. However, linguistic nationalism was high in the context of an antagonistic view towards Hindi. The camp propagating the continued usage of English was one with strong anti-Hindi sentiments, rather than a strong pro-English one. An alternative to using English that could have been fostered was the promotion and development of regional languages to make them wholesome education mediums. However, this alternative path was not adopted, and instead the consolidation of English was pursued. This consolidation further connected the education system of India with the English language.

The question that arises is why did India, in the past 72 years, not cultivate its numerous regional languages to make them quality educational mediums, instead of continuously using English? The process of developing regional languages, though a herculean task, could have surely taken huge strides forward in 72 years. Moreover, the pursuit of such a task could have appeased linguistic nationalistic sentiments of the diverse population. Macaulay's prediction that Indians well acquainted with western knowledge and science would enrich and help "raise up a good vernacular literature in the country" within 20 years due to their "inclination and the ability to exhibit European knowledge in the vernacular dialects"[56] did not come true; instead of enriching native languages, India took a complete inclination towards English.

The answer is simple – the demand for English speakers, rather than indigenous language speakers, increased in India, thereby increasing the grasp of the language on the country. The amalgamated reasons for the increase in this demand are twofold – one global and the other internal. Demand for English speakers has increased because of the United States of America's economic supremacy accompanied by globalisation (global factor), and India's dependence on its service sector (local factor). In other words, in contemporary India, the reason for the persistence of the western language is no longer limited to education and administration. It has now disseminated into the economy.

The United States of America's economic supremacy and globalisation

As David Crystal rightly argues, it may take a politically and militarily strong nation to establish a language, but it takes an economically powerful nation to maintain and expand it.[57] During the twentieth century, the country with the dominant economic might was the United States of America, with native English speakers. By extension of Crystal's theory, the USA's economic might assured the consolidation and expansion of the English language on a global scale, including in India, after Britain had established it.

The impetus of the USA's economic might perpetuating into language dominance globally was aided extensively by the fact that, during the same time-period as its economic reign, the world opened up. The USA's economic progress was simultaneously accompanied with globalisation. Economic developments began to operate on a global scale and were supported by new communication technologies including telegraph, telephone, radio and email. What followed was the development and fostering of big multinational organisations operating across borders in numerous countries. The growth of globally competitive industries paved the way for new levels of international marketing and advertisement that were never seen before. Broadcasting media and press, with electromagnetic ease, crossed national borders. Add to this the avenue opened by the internet, and we had entered a world in which cross-border communication started taking place quickly. International broadcasts of television shows and movies exposed to the indigenous populations of foreign nations the culture of the US, especially the language. This new mass entertainment industry had a worldwide impact. Increase in the world demand for more scientific research and development paved the way for a culture of international education, with institutions opening up for further education. Social media platforms provided the impetus to break cross-border walls that were evident up until a decade back.

Given that the US was the most productive and fastest growing economy during this period of rapid globalisation, its language, English, benefited the most from this explosion of international activities. That the country housed (and continues to house) prominent higher education and research institutions, mass media and production companies, and social media platforms further added to the country's – and axiomatically its language's – outreach. Therefore, while British political imperialism sent English across the globe, including India, it was US economic supremacy aided by globalisation that consolidated this expansion in the twentieth and twenty-first centuries. Globally, economics replaced politics as the driving factor behind the dominance of the English language, and the same trend got replicated in India. The country's dependence on English was no longer circumscribed to political and institutional factors. In order to prosper from the benefits associated with globalisation accompanied by US economic supremacy, India had to become further reliant on the English language.

Service-driven growth in India

It is common knowledge that in this era of globalisation, familiarity with English – the famously recognised global language – has become an additional (if not necessary) skill to possess. It is safe to assume that the language can enable individuals and nations to enhance their economic returns by providing increased access to people and businesses outside national boundaries. Nonetheless, despite this logical supposition, countries such as China and Japan have managed to prosper from economic benefits without depending on the western language to the same degree as India. In fact, in the decade post-1991, during which India prospered from rapid economic growth averaging 7.5%, China performed better, averaging a Gross Domestic Product of 9.8%.[58] The China story evidently shows that a country's economy can prosper without relying extensively on the English language, despite the momentum it causes through globalisation.

Given that the two premises – first, India could have gradually shifted to regional languages in the past 69 years had its reliance on English only been limited to administration and education arenas; and second, English is not a necessary condition for prosperity in the economic arena in this era of globalisation as substantiated by China – the question that arises is why did India continue relying on English to such an inelastic level? The answer lies in the path of growth followed by India.

Contrary to China, whose post-1993 growth acceleration was concentrated on the manufacturing sector, which contributed nearly 60% of the country's aggregate productivity growth,[59] India's growth was service driven. Approximately 45% of India's growth post-1993 was accounted for by the service sector of the economy.[60] In fiscal year 2009–2010, services accounted for 57.3% of India's GDP, while the average for the decade 2000–2010 was 53.7%.[61] Barry Bosworth, Susan M. Collins and Arvind Virmani, taking the 1999–2000 growth figures of India, highlighted that seven services constituted 41% of the total GDP during the fiscal year and were therefore largely responsible for India's growth. These seven services included Trade, Communication, Transport and Storage, Banking and Insurance, Hotels and Restaurants, Real Estate and Business Services, and Public Administration and Defence – with Trade in services alone constituting 12.9% of the GDP.[62] Arpita Mukherjee, in her 2013 paper, corroborated these findings by analysing the National Income Accounts (Ministry of Statistics and Programme Implementation) for the time-period 2000–2010 and concluded that these seven sub-services constituted 45.7% of the GDP (see Table 2.3).

There exists an inherent dependency of a service-driven economy on the English language capabilities of its workforce, particularly in the multilingual India. This is substantiated by the works of Mehtabul Azam, Aimee Chin and Nishith Prakash, who highlighted that English-speaking skills were more widespread in those districts of India that had an information technology firm in 2003 – which can be construed as a proxy for service sector firms. The authors quantified that in districts with an IT firm presence, 30% of the population is English speaking (7.7% fluent speakers and 22.3% partial speakers). On the other hand, in districts with no IT form presence, only 16.9% of the population is English speaking (2.6% fluent speakers and 14.3% partial speakers).

Table 2.3 Distribution of India's GDP by sector

Industry	*Fiscal Year: 1999–2000*	*Decadal Average: 2000–2010*
Agriculture and allied	25.3	21.8
Manufacturing/Industry	25.4	24.5
Services	49.2	53.7
Trade	*12.9*	*14.3*
Hotel and restaurants	*1.2*	*1.4*
Transport and storage	*5.8*	*6.5*
Communication	*1.6*	*2.8*
Banking and insurance	*5.9*	*6.5*
Real Estate, ownership of swellings and business services	*7.1*	*8.2*
Public administration and defence	*6.7*	*6.0*
Sub-service total	41	45.7
Other services	8.1	8.0
Total	100.0	100.0

Source: The 1999–2000 data has been sourced from Bosworth, Collins, and Virmani (2007), while the average decadal data is from Mukherjee (2013).

To further understand the role and relevance of the English language in the service sector, I conducted interviews with large, medium and small firms belonging to the aforementioned seven service sector industries that have been credited with growing India's economy. It must be noted here that, while I incorporated different sizes of the firms within the sectors, the individual interviewees were all management level or above. The reason for this upwardly skewed selection of respondents stems from the rationale for the interviews. The interviews were largely to understand the relevance of the language in the service sector relative to other sectors – incorporating both in-house as well as customer demand for the language. Thus, those at a decision-making capacity were assumed to be more likely to provide holistic answers. The evident deduction of the interviews were the two potential reasons explaining why a service-driven economy like India depends more on the global language of English than a manufacturing based country.

The first reason stems from the fact that English is the language of communication with the clients in the service sector. Service industries, being predominantly client facing, perceptibly utilise language and communication more than the physical manufacturing sector. In agriculture and manufacturing industries, clients care for products and goods that are largely tangible. If the product or good delivered is quality, all else matters little. In services, on the other hand, one's communication with the client becomes a good in itself. May it be in real estate, where firms and clients' correspondences are based on documents written in English, such as by-laws and purchase orders, or hotels, where good interactions with guests assures quality service and customer retention, communication is not only a crucial driver but is also one of the ultimate deliverables.

It is consequently essential that the firms in these sectors be well versed in the language of communication in which its clients are most conformable. Since most of the firms belonging to these service industries span across states within India as well as across borders (in terms of their operations and/or service delivery), the clients are not circumscribed to Hindi speakers. As rightly stated by a member of a renowned chamber of commerce and industries in India,

> one needs to be able to converse with clients who are not only from North India when providing services. In a country where indigenous language, or lingo, changes every few kilometres, it would be irrational to expect a firm to communicate with clients in their regional languages. Since English-speaking skills are more spread out and dispersed across India relative to Hindi, it makes sense to use English while providing services.[63]

Furthermore, the clientele of these firms is not limited to the Indian border. Industries such as hotels and restaurants, transport and storage, and trade in services have frequent dealings with foreign clientele who are predominantly English speakers. Similarly, officers in the public administration and defence sector have to often interact with foreign delegations in the wake of joint exercises and exchange programmes.

Since the clients require these service providers to converse with them in English, these service providers in turn require their staff and hired workers to be fluent in the language. This opinion, shared unanimously by all respondents, is substantiated by an apt quote by a manager at a capital advisory company – "if there is a choice to be made between two people having the exact same qualifications, the individual who is able to interact with the client better by knowing English will be chosen as client satisfaction is of utmost importance."[64]

The second reason for the dependence of services, relative to other sectors, on the English language generates from the fact that the said language is a medium of knowledge absorption and diffusion. In the service sector, language becomes an important means of absorbing a stock of knowledge. In defence, for instance, literature and user guides on equipment are in English. In the real estate sector, firms deal with documents written in English including contracts, by-laws, purchase orders, designs, architectural drawings and bills. A potential reason for this dependence on English to absorb knowledge stems from the fact that prominently established knowledge has been generated outside of the country, and almost always in English, owing to India's relatively less developed manufacturing and R&D sectors. While notable efforts have been made in recent years to enhance the country's manufacturing, the noteworthy results of this expansion will inevitably come with a lag. So far, Indian services have had to rely on knowledge created elsewhere in English, as evidenced by the response from a manager in the banking and insurance sector:

> Look at mobile banking for instance. We adopted the idea and most of our clients use smartphones created in the United States. All this information was provided to us in English. Even when knowledge is created in India these days, it is almost always in English, and that's how we absorb it. We can make domestic smartphones, but large number of the users of these phones rely on the English for usage of the product.[65]

Additionally, the language plays a crucial role in diffusing knowledge within the firms. In agriculture and manufacturing, one can show and, axiomatically, teach their staff how to produce the commodity at hand. In services, though knowledge diffusion for execution level staff can be done through display, the most important jobs are the client-facing ones that require diffusion of knowledge via verbal communication. A corroboration of this is fittingly provided by the Group Head of a chain of hotels in India:

> I can show a cleaner how to improve the cleaning, but I have to communicate with my Duty Manager on how to correct and recover for service failure. For instance, we provide training through scripts in English to our front of house (FOH) staff on what to say to a client in case of potential service failure.[66]

In this regard, English not only becomes a medium of absorption and diffusion of knowledge in the service sector, but it also becomes explicit knowledge in itself.

Given that the service sector of India serves a vast clientele across India and the world, English has become the most convenient and essential choice for communication. The fact that the country's manufacturing base and R&D is relatively less competitive on a global scale, the stock of knowledge for the service sector is usually adapted (for instance, from academic journals and equipment manuals) through the medium of English. Furthermore, the service sector has been influenced greatly by globalisation, with increases in cross-border trade, foreign direct investment, cross-country mergers and international joint ventures that have augmented the number of multinational service enterprises.[67] All this has led to an increase in the demand for English speakers in the job market of India. This can be corroborated by the 2013 report by Aspiring Minds, India's leading employability solutions company, which concluded that

47% of graduates are not employable in any sector of the knowledge economy because of their lack of English language and cognitive skills.

To add to the already dependent administrative and educational institutions of India, contemporary India's economy has also now become intertwined with the English language. The demand for English speakers in the economy has grown, with English proficiency becoming a criterion for high paid jobs and good wage returns. While the supply of English speakers is gradually increasing to meet this demand, the average number of English speakers is still troublingly low.

Seven reasons for the persistent prevalence of the English language

The English language entered India with British colonialism and automatically became a symbol of elitism. It remained in India in the years following independence because of high anti-Hindi sentiments in the multilingual country whose constitution was laid out by English-speaking *babus*. This anti-Hindi sentiment, accompanied by the fact that the education system of India had, for 112 years, been influenced by western knowledge through the medium of English, became instrumental in consolidating the language's grasp on the educational system of the country. As years passed by, more knowledge was created with ease of dispersion in the twentieth century due to globalisation. The country leading the R&D and productivity race was the United States of America, whose native language happened to be English. India over these years created and manufactured less, and they instead concentrated on services. Providing services to a multilingual clientele in the era of globalisation further paved the way for the consolidation of the western language, and the result was high demand and wage returns for English speakers in the job market of India. One must keep in mind that this is a country that had, throughout its history, attached a value of elitism to the language, thereby making its speakers perceivably superior. In contemporary India, that superiority is reflected in the wages.

Through this historical analysis of the English language in India over the years, the complex reasoning behind the dominating and persistent prevalence of the language, despite the fact that a mere 28.7% Indians speak it, can be summarised into seven factors:

1. The elite value attached to the language, which has manifested into economic value over the years.
2. Linguistic heterogeneity of the country and anti-Hindi sentiments.
3. The geographic dispersion of English speakers within India relative to the geographic concentration of the Hindi speakers.
4. Globalisation.
5. US economic supremacy.

6 India's service-driven growth.
7 Relative lack of created knowledge, and dependence on western knowledge that requires a medium of absorption.

All these factors, phased in at different points in time throughout history, have compositely made English a necessity for India's political, educational and economic functioning. Furthermore, though the supply of English speakers is still below average, the number has been gradually increasing over the years. With this gradual increase in the number of English speakers to meet the high demand, it would be reasonable to say that the English language might continue sustaining its hegemony in India. Nevertheless, regardless of its future, we can encapsulate the reason for the continuous consolidated presence of English in India using David Crystal's words: it was in the right place at the right time.

Notes

1 Retrieved August 13, 2018, from www.columbia.edu/itc/mealac/pritchett/00generallinks/macaulay/txt_minute_education_1835.html
2 Crystal, *English as a global language*.
3 Vermani, R. C. (2000). *Colonialism and nationalism in India*. New Delhi: Gitanjali Publishing House.
4 This view propagates that British colonialism of India was simply a foreign rule, and not an economic, political and social structure that was exploitative.
5 According to this view, which was advanced as a justification for European colonialism, it was the presumed responsibility of white people to "'civilise" and govern the non-white people.
6 This view emphasises that the British rule was essentially benevolent, as it formed a stage that paved the way for India's self-government.
7 This school of thought views colonialism as an exploitative structure.
8 This approach propagates that underprivileged and marginalised masses in colonial India viewed their colonisers as a triad of government, moneylenders and landowners.
9 Ghosh, S. C. (1995). Bentinck, Macaulay and the introduction of English education in India. *History of Education*, *24*(1), 17–24. Retrieved from www.tandfonline.com/doi/abs/10.1080/0046760950240102?journalCode=thed20
10 In Tully, M. (1997). English: An advantage to India? *English Language Teaching Journal*, *51*(2), 151–164.
11 A practice of self-immolation of a widow on the funeral pyre of her husband.
12 In Sharp, H. (1920). *Selections from educational records: 1781–1839* (Part 1). Calcutta: Government Printing Press.
13 Ghosh, Bentinck, Macaulay and the introduction of English education in India.
14 Sharp, *Selections from Educational Records: 1781–1839* (Part 1).
15 Ibid.
16 In Ghosh, Bentinck, Macaulay and the introduction of English education in India.
17 Embree, A. T. (1962). *Charles Grant and British rule in India*. London: Allen & Unwin.
18 Kochhar, R. (2008). Seductive orientalism: English education and modern science in colonial India. *Social Scientist*, *36*, 53–57.

19 In Ghosh, Bentinck, Macaulay and the introduction of English education in India.
20 Winch, D. (1966). Editor's introduction. In Winch, D. (Eds.), *James Mill: Selected economic writings*. Edinburgh: Oliver Boyd for the Scottish Economic Society.
21 Mill, J. (1826). *The history of British India*. London: Baldwin, Cradock and Joy.
22 Majeed, J. (1990). James Mill's "The history of British India" and utilitarianism as a rhetoric of reform. *Modern Asian Studies*, *24*(2), 209–224.
23 Mill, *The history of British India*.
24 It is worth noting that Mill's utilitarianism was different from Bentham's. While the former associated utilitarianism with usefulness, the latter explained it in terms of pleasure.
25 Mantena, K. (2007). The crisis of liberal imperialism. in Bell, D. (Ed.), *Victorian visions of global order: Empire and international relations in nineteenth-century political thought*. Cambridge: Cambridge University Press.
26 Sharp, *Selections from educational records: 1781–1839* (Part 1).
27 In Tully, English: An advantage to India?
28 In Sharp, *Selections from educational records: 1781–1839* (Part 1).
29 In Ghosh, Bentinck, Macaulay and the introduction of English education in India.
30 Ibid.
31 Ibid.
32 In Tully, English: An advantage to India?
33 Ibid.
34 Spear, T. G. P. (1938). Bentinck and education. *Cambridge Historical Journal*, *VI*, 78–101.
35 In Bowring, J. (1843). *The works of Jeremy Bentham*. London. In Ghosh, Bentinck, Macaulay and the introduction of English education in India.
36 Ghosh, Bentinck, Macaulay and the introduction of English education in India.
37 Acts of organised gangs of robbers and murderers who operated in the Indian subcontinent. The English word "thug" originates from here.
38 In Ghosh, Bentinck, Macaulay and the introduction of English education in India.
39 Ibid.
40 Ibid.
41 Mayhew, A. (1926). *The education of India*. London: Faber & Gwyer.
42 In Young, G. M. (1967). *Macaulay: Prose and poetry*. London: Hart-Davis.
43 Raina, B. (1994). A note on language, and the politics of English in India. In S. Joshi (Ed.), *Rethinking English: Essays in literature, language, history* (pp. 265–297). New Delhi: Oxford University Press.
44 Electronic version of Macaulay's minute. Retrieved from www.columbia.edu/itc/mealac/pritchett/00generallinks/macaulay/txt_minute_education_1835.html
45 British Library. (2014). *Indian national congress*. Retrieved August 15, 2015, from www.bl.uk/reshelp/findhelpregion/asia/india/indianindependence/indiannat/source1/index.html
46 Ibid.
47 Aggarwal, J. C. (2007). *Landmarks in the history of modern Indian education* (6th ed.). New Delhi: Vikas Publishing House Private Limited.
48 Government of India. (1953). *Report of the secondary education commission*. New Delhi: Ministry of Education.
49 All Gov India. (2017). *Department of official language*. Retrieved August 10, 2018, from www.allgov.com/india/departments/ministry-of-home-affairs/department-of-official-language?agencyid=7577

50 In Dakin, J., Tiffen, B., and Widdowsom, H. G. (1968). *Language in education: The problem in commonwealth Africa and the Indo-Pakistan subcontinent.* London: Oxford University Press.
51 All Gov India, *Department of official language.*
52 Ibid.
53 Azam, M., Chin, A., and Prakash, N. (2011). The returns to English-language skills in India. *Economic Development and Cultural Change, 61*(2), 335–367.
54 Ibid.
55 The 2005 figures are adapted from Azam, Chin and Prakash's work "The returns to English-language skills in India" (2011), which has used the India Human Development Survey Round 1. The 2011 figures have been tabulated using the India Human Development Survey Round 2. The sample for both the years include individuals aged 18–65.
56 In Sharp, *Selections from educational records: 1781–1839* (Part 1).
57 Crystal, *English as a global language.*
58 Lin, J. Y. (2013, August 5). Long live China's boom. *Project Syndicate.* Retrieved March 11, 2018, from www.project-syndicate.org/commentary/growth-and-the-chinese-economy-s-latecomer-advantage-by-justin-yifu-lin
59 Ibid. Though it was recently reported that China is now transitioning from manufacturing to services as growth slows (*The Wall Street Journal*, 2016).
60 Bosworth, B., Collins, S. M., and Virmani, A. (2007). Sources of growth in the Indian economy. *India Policy Forum, 3*, 1–50; Eichengreen, B., and Gupta, P. (2011). *The service sector as India's road to economic growth.* National Bureau of Economic Research Working Paper no. 16757.
61 Mukherjee, A. (2013). *The service sector in India.* ADB Economics Working Paper Series, 352.
62 The classification of services included in this sector is provided in Appendix 2.
63 Qualitative finding revealed during primary data collection. The name of the respondent has been kept anonymous as per request.
64 Qualitative finding revealed during primary data collection. The name of the respondent has been kept anonymous as per request.
65 Qualitative finding revealed during primary data collection. The name of the respondent has been kept anonymous as per request.
66 It is worth noting that within these service sector organisations, workers are generally divided into two groups – the execution level staff and client-facing staff. The execution level positions are the low paid jobs, and workers belonging to this tier generally do not communicate with the clients and are therefore not required to be fluent in English. Examples of execution level staff include drivers, warehouse labour, sorting staff, forklift or crane operators in the transport and storage industry, construction workers in the real estate industry, housekeepers and cleaners in the hospitality industry, et al. It is the client-facing jobs, or the front-of-house (FOH) jobs that get the maximum salary returns. These staff members are the ones required to be proficient in English.
67 For more details on the impact of globalisation on the service sectors, read G. Hufbauer and T. Warren (1999). *The globalization of services: What has happened? What are the implications?* Working Paper Series WP99-12.

3

THE ENGLISH LANGUAGE AND ECONOMIC GROWTH

Language-growth relationship: a theoretical framework

> *English is critical for countries' successful participation in the global economy . . . it provides individuals with access to crucial knowledge, skills and employment opportunities and enables organisations to create and sustain international links.*
>
> – (Hywel Coleman, 2011)

The previous chapter considered the reasons for the prevalence of the English language in India, stressing on the persistency of it. For the same, a brief picture was provided about the dissemination of the dominance of English in the economic arena – specifically, how, due to India's legacy, service sector dependency and the existing era of globalisation, proficiency in the global language of English has become a necessary skill to possess in the labour market of the country. The language increases access to people and businesses outside the national boundary, and assumedly permits the English-speaking labour force of India to escalate their economic returns. While we can reasonably state that the language paves the way for an increase in returns at the *individual* level, it wouldn't be unreasonable to hypothesise, by extension, that it may yield returns at the *national* level. In other words, English language proficiency might have a positive relationship with the economic growth rate of India.

To validate this statement, a theoretical underpinning is mandatory. What is equally necessary – though some might disagree – is an empirical backing to appease my fellow hard-line economists. In this chapter, I attempt to do both, starting with an explanation of the theoretical dynamics that shape the language-growth relationship. Before diving deep into the empirical estimations, I cede that this section of the book, for the sake of academic rigour, faces a trade-off with generalist narrative for wider consumption. While I attempt to keep the narrative simple, for non-economists, certain sections of this chapter may contain jargon.

When I first started researching this topic back in 2012,[1] much to my luck, a paper by Chew Ging Lee, Professor of Quantitative Methods at the University of Nottingham, was published. This paper, titled "English Language and Economic Growth: Cross-Country Empirical Evidence,"[2] was a seminal work that addressed empirically the language-growth relationship. It also became the work that provided an academically sound base to explain a relationship that was largely based on presumed experiential knowledge. According to Lee, this basis stems from the widely accepted knowledge-growth relationship.

It is common wisdom that accumulation of knowledge by a country has a positive impact on the economic growth of the country. Knowledge creation through firms' R&D initiatives in particular, is a noteworthy factor behind increasing growth.[3] Alternatively, getting secondary access to this newly created knowledge can also escalate growth.[4]

At a given time, the amount of knowledge that a country possesses, or the existing stock of knowledge, can be increased and enhanced either through the creation of new knowledge via investment in R&D, or through access of knowledge founded in other countries. It is widely accepted that developed countries possess the capabilities to adopt the former technique, and indeed it is empirically evident that the majority of new knowledge is created by these developed countries in which the English language enjoys a special status. Research also dictates that developing countries enjoy efficiency gains if they adopt the knowledge created in developed countries. Consequently, developing countries, which lack the means (may they be financial means or human resource means or others) to invest in knowledge creation, must predominantly pursue the access and absorption technique to increase their stock of knowledge for efficiency gains and the subsequent growth.

Lee, citing Wolfgang Keller,[5] suggested that newly created knowledge through R&D in the developed countries can be transmitted to developing countries by increasing economic integration and initiating new means of telecommunication. Such a transmission would ensure that people in all countries have access to the same stock of knowledge. For this spillover and diffusion of knowledge to happen from one economy to the other effectively, there needs to be transference capabilities amongst the developed countries and absorptive capabilities amongst the developing countries. Globalisation has enabled economic integration to a large extent, thereby opening the door for international knowledge spillover. The area of concentration now is the medium through which this knowledge can be diffused by the developed countries and absorbed by the developing countries. This medium is the global language English.

Regardless of what we use as the proxy for new knowledge, may it be internationally accepted journals or machinery instruction manuals, the role of the English language has become eminent in spreading it. Lee provides convincing examples to substantiate the importance of English in disseminating knowledge. One such example is academic journals, including those published in non-English-speaking developed countries. These include the *German Economic Review*, the official publication of the German Economic Association (Verein für Socialpolitik), and the *Spanish Economic Review*, the official publication of the Spanish Economic Association (Asociación Española de Economía), which are both published in English. Even *Konjunkturpolitik* relaunched itself in 2003, after publishing 49 volumes with German articles. Today, it is the *Applied Economics Quarterly*, which publishes exclusively in English.[6]

Even if we shift our focus to the impact of English on daily activities, we notice that machineries usually come with instruction manuals in English. Without a basic understanding of the language, workers will be unable to use these machines productively. Lee suggested that the language of communication among R&D engineers in Germany and Italy could be English at the manufacturing industry level. Based on these examples, it would be unwise to deny that individuals are more likely to get access to the new knowledge if they have English proficiency.[7] Ergo, the dynamics of the language-growth relationship are summarised in Figure 3.1.

In other words, since more knowledge implies higher growth, more English language proficiency in developing countries, including India – that largely rely on access through absorption methodology for increasing their stock of knowledge – axiomatically implies higher growth. In this regard, the stock of knowledge becomes the conduit through which the language, as a part of human capital, influences growth.

It is important to note that not *all* developing countries follow the "access through absorption" path in the earlier framework to increase their stock of knowledge and resultant growth. English language proficiency is, therefore, not an essential criterion for their growth. An example of one such developing nation is China.

China is a developing country with a large fraction of non-English speakers, approximating 99%[8] – substantially higher than India's 71.3%. If they followed the "access through absorption" path in the earlier framework, their stock of knowledge and the subsequent economic growth should have been at a disadvantage. However, their growth, averaging 9.8% in the past three decades,[9] was higher than that of India's, or of most countries for that matter. It is therefore imperative to specify that the *path of growth* and the *type of knowledge* are essential considerations for the empirical applicability of this framework.

In China, the post-1993 growth acceleration was concentrated mostly in industry, which contributed nearly 60% of China's aggregate productivity growth. In contract, as stated previously, India's post-1993 growth was

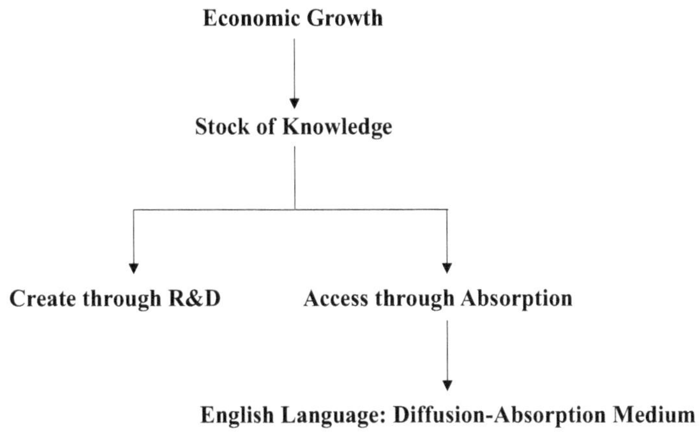

Figure 3.1 Relationship between English language and economic growth

Source: Theory adapted from Lee (2012).

largely service driven. While Barry Bosworth, Susan M. Collins and Arvind Virmani credited Communication, Transport and Storage, Banking and Insurance, Hotels and Restaurants, Real Estate and Business Services, and Public Administration and Defence Services for the growth (see Table 2.3), Barry Eichengreen and Poonam Gupta credited services including Financial Intermediation, Computer Services, Business Services, Communications, and Legal and Technical services. For most of these services, the English language is not only a medium for knowledge diffusion, but it is also explicit knowledge itself. Therefore, the earlier framework applies predominantly to countries whose service sector growth explains the economic growth, such as India.

In other words, the relationship between the English language and economic growth is evident in those countries who have two enabling conditions: first, the stock of knowledge must be dependent on the absorption methodology, rather than through investment in R&D, and; second, the economies must be primarily service driven.

Language-growth relationship around the globe

Most economies are increasingly powered by trade, which represented 56% of world GDP in 2015, up from 44% in 1995. Overwhelmingly, the common language required for these global transactions is English.

– (EF English Proficiency Index Report, 2018)

The theoretical and positive language-growth correlation lacks in depth empirical underpinning, though recent years have seen an increasing interest in this area of research. Most research concentrations in this area have yielded a similar narrative – there predominantly exists a positive correlation between the English language and the economic performance of countries, even if causality cannot be determined.

Education First (EF), an international education company, in their 2018 English Proficiency Index,[10] allocated 88 countries into five proficiency bands ranging from Very High to Very Low. This ranking was based on test data from more than 1,300,000 test takers around the world who took the EF Standard English Test (EF SET) in 2017. While Sweden ranked 1st with Very High proficiency, India ranked 28th, falling in the Moderate proficiency bracket. China gained the 47th rank with Low Proficiency. Traditionally, proficiency of a country must encompass two lenses – number of speakers in a country and the ability of the speakers (i.e. fluent versus little). Since EF English Proficiency Index only captures the latter lens, its ranking can be construed as circumscribed to the subset of established English-speakers. Nonetheless, what is of interest is the correlation that Education First establishes between the English Proficiency Index and key economic indicators, including gross domestic product (GDP) and average gross income across these countries. Their report highlights a positive relationship between the two, with the countries falling in the High Proficiency bracket displaying highest GDP, and vice versa.

Validating the theoretical framework presented in the previous chapter, the report states that the reason for this positive language-growth relationship stems from the transition of developing countries from agriculture or manufacturing to a knowledge-based economic model. The latter requires skilled adults who are "able to sell their services internationally."[11] Accordingly, the report finds a strong correlation between English proficiency and service exports.

The limitation of an as-is correlation, however, is that it does not capture the other variables that could be explaining the high economic performance of English proficient countries, such as education level and the region-specific context. Additionally, let us not overlook the endogeneity problem – simply put, are GDP and average gross income higher because English competency is high, or is English competency higher because GDP and average gross income is high?

Two academically rigorous cross-country studies were conducted in 2012 and 2013 – by Chew Ging Lee, and Jean Louis Arcand and Francois Grin, respectively – to understand the empirics of this language-growth relationship. Lee's 2012 paper concluded that the outstanding growth of Asian countries, including India, could be attributed to the large investment in the enhancement of human capital that fosters English-speaking culture and "promotes a climate of the use of English."[12] On the other hand, Arcand and Grin concluded that competence in English is not associated with GDP per capita. While difference in methodology, as well as the scholars' differing proxy for English proficiency,[13] can be examined to explain the opposing findings, I believe it is more pertinent to accept rather than deconstruct this contradiction. The English language may have a positive association with economic growth in certain regional and periodic contexts. It is reasonable to accept that the positive relationship might not be a global phenomenon owing to varying local contexts.

To date, and to my awareness, the aforementioned studies are the only two that have empirically studied the effect of English language on growth. Nevertheless, work has been done to highlight the role of the language in influencing other economic indicators that in turn determine growth. These indictors include wages at an *individual* level, amount of business at the *industrial* level and congruency of language policies and economic policies at the *national* level.

Francois Grin's 2003 paper, titled *English as Economic Values: Facts and Fallacies*, concentrated on the individual level by studying the labour market value of English language skills in Switzerland. The results indicated that, in Switzerland, English language skills could be associated with remarkably high and statistically robust wage premia that ranged from 12%to 30%.[14] These noteworthy returns exist despite English being neither a majority nor an official language in the country. It is only rational, and empirically correct, to construe that the positively high and robust language-earnings association would be further imbedded in countries, such as India, where English serves as a national and/or official language.

Mehtabul Azam, Aimee Chin and Nishith Prakash, in *The Returns to English-Language Skills in India*, found that there are large and statistically significant returns to English language skills in the country. Their paper concluded that per hour wages in India are on average 34% higher for men with fluent English-speaking skills and 13% higher for men with little English-speaking skills relative to men who speak no English. For women, the average returns are 22% for fluent English speakers and 10% for partial English speakers relative to non-speakers.[15]

In *Traditional Institutions Meet the Modern World: Caste, Gender, and Schooling Choice in a Globalizing Economy*, Kaivan Munshi and Mark Rosenzweig collected their own data on Maharashtrians living in Dadar, an area in Mumbai, Maharashtra, India. Using data on parents' income histories and the language of instruction in their secondary schools (Marathi or English), they approximated significant positive returns to an English-medium education. According to their study, attending an English-medium school increased both women's and men's incomes by about 25% in 2000.

Tanika Chakraborty and Shilpi Kapur Bakshi, in their unpublished manuscript of 2008 titled *English Language Premium: Evidence from a Policy Experiment in India*, used National Sample Survey data to estimate the impact of a 1983 policy in West Bengal that removed English as the medium of instruction in primary schools. They found that switching from English to Bengali as the medium of instruction significantly reduced wages. Simple comparisons of cohorts attending primary school before and after the policy change suggested that English-medium schooling raised wages by approximately 15% in the 2000s.[16]

The scholars published a paper in 2015 with the same title as their previous manuscript, in which they highlighted that a 10% lower probability of learning English in primary schools in India leads to a decline in weekly wages by 8%. On an average, this implies 26% lower wages for cohorts exposed to the policy change.

At the industrial/firm level, while no literature addressed the case of India, Ford and Strange in their 1999 article *Where do Japanese Manufacturing Firms Invest in Europe, and Why?* showed that Japanese manufacturing firms take into consideration English speaking ability of the potential host countries when making decisions about where to establish manufacturing affiliates.[17] In other words, a work force possessing English language skills is an attractive feature for multinationals seeking new locations. Therefore, the economy of a country emphasising English would prosper by attracting larger foreign direct investment.

Hywel Coleman in *The English Language in Development* suggested that a country based on the service sector and manufacturing sector – in that order – should be more dependent on English, as it is needed for the benefit of the economy. And indeed, India requires English, as its growth is dependent on the service sector. However, Coleman added that a country with a majority of its population belonging to the agricultural sector should not stress extensively on this global language, or else the language could become a "means of barring access to the less privileged."[18] Indeed, this is the case in India where, according to Census 2011, 61.5% of the population belongs to the agricultural sector and cannot extract the economic and monetary benefits of the global language. India's English dependent service-driven growth, accompanied by the non-English-speaking, agriculture-based population, provides an explanation for the highly non-inclusive growth. This will be discussed in detail in the next section of the book.

In *Does English rule? Language instruction and economic strategies in Singapore, Ireland and Puerto Rico*, Suárez concentrated on the national level by using a cross-country framework. The study investigated the relationship between countries' economic policies and language education policies by comparing Singapore, Ireland and Puerto Rico – all relatively small island nations with strong export oriented economies but with very different national language policies. The work concluded that Singapore had achieved a high level of congruence between its language education policy and economic policies, where all subjects are taught in English. On the other hand, Puerto Rico – where teacher unions refused to adopt English as the teaching medium – was concluded to have a low level of policy congruence. The research concluded that "countries pursuing an economic strategy based on exports and the attraction of foreign capital should adapt their language education policies to the requirements of that economic strategy."[19] India is the 19th largest exporter, and 13th largest importer in the world.[20] Thus, this study by extension implies that, at a macro level, English is very much essential for good economic performance in India.

These global empirics illustrate that the positive association between the English language and economic indicators is more than just a theoretical concept. Its practical applicability is evident, even if it is not universally true. The English language largely correlates with economic growth, either directly or indirectly, through its impact on wages and foreign investment. Yet the conclusions from Jean Louis Arcand and Francois Grin's work cannot be overlooked, and the empirics of this relationship must be deconstructed within regional and/or periodic circumscription. With this is mind, and to address the evident gap in the literature pertaining to the language-growth relationship in the Indian context, let us move ahead to test a hypothesis – is English language ability positively correlated to economic growth in India?

How many of us can speak it?

India's first minister of education Maulana Azad wrote: "One thing is quite clear and definite, and I have no doubt that any Indian will disagree with me. The position English occupies . . . in our educational and official life cannot be sustained in future." He couldn't foresee that in future Indians would, in fact, quite disagree with him.

– (Sreetilak Sambhanda, 2018)[21]

Prior to investigating the link between the English language and economic indicators in India, one must analyse the distribution of English speakers across various categories. This section provides the said distribution using the Indian Human Development Survey Round 2, which is the latest available data on English proficiency.

As discussed in Chapter 2 of this book, India is a linguistically diverse nation with thousands of languages, out of which, according to the 2001 census, 122 have over 10,000 speakers. English ranks 44th on the list of languages with the most native speakers in the country. Yet the importance of English as the language of power and prestige cannot be undermined, thanks to the legacy that the British left behind that spanned over administration, education and law. The calls to replace English with a native language post-independence proved to be infeasible, since the primary candidate, Hindi, was politically opposed by a large fraction of the country. Therefore, the Indian Constitution names both English and Hindi as the official languages of the country and, while individual states legislate their own official languages, communication in the federal government and among states is conducted in English and Hindi.

At an individual level, it wouldn't be unreasonable to assume that there are economic benefits to knowing English. The first benefit arises from the value associated with English as the lingua franca in this multilingual country, where the local languages divide people and a foreign language unites people. This value is further extended when we expand the market scope from the country to the world. The second benefit arises from the value English possesses due to its positioning in government and educational institutions. The attractive white-collar occupations of India that provide secure employment and good benefits, such as high-level government officials and school teachers, are reserved for the English speakers. The non-English speakers, on the other hand, predominantly remain in the agricultural sector or casual labour jobs, which yield relatively uncertain wages and livelihoods.

It is therefore understandable why India has seen an increase in the number of English speakers over the years. In 2001, 12% of the population reported having English-speaking ability, as a first, second or third language, according to the census data. In 2005, the figure rose to 20%, of which 4%spoke fluently while the remaining spoke partially.[22] To obtain and tabulate the latest figures for the number of English speakers in India, I have used IHDS Round 2, with a nationally representative weighted sample of 729,428,794.

Table 3.1 provides the average English ability among individuals aged 18–65 in the IHDS Round 2 along various dimensions. Only 28.7% of the population reported as having some English proficiency. This figure is comprised of approximately 6.3% who can converse fluently in English and 22.4% who can converse a little in English. English ability in India is higher among men. Approximately 35.1% of men reported having English-speaking ability as compared to 22.6% of women. This difference can be a result of the differences in educational attainment between the two genders. The language speaking ability is also higher among younger people, as 36.4% of people aged 18–35 reported having English-speaking proficiency while only 18.6% of people aged 51–65 reported the same. This difference may be due to globalisation as well as the inclination towards service sector jobs over agriculture in recent decades.

English-speaking ability increases rapidly with educational attainment in the country. Eighty-nine percent of individuals with a college degree (minimum being a bachelor's degree) have English-speaking capabilities as compared to 63% for those with secondary school qualification with ten to 14 years of

Table 3.1 Percentage of English speakers in India (2011)

	Percentage of Indians with Fluent English Ability(1)	*Percentage of Indians with Little English Ability(2)*	*Total Percentage of Indians with English Ability(3) = (1) + (2)*
All Individual Aged 18–65	6.3	22.4	28.7
By Gender			
Male	8.0	27.0	35.0
Female	4.7	17.9	22.6
By Age			
18–35	8.1	28.3	36.4
36–50	4.5	16.5	21.0
51–65	4.2	14.4	18.6
By Educational Attainment			
No Completed Schooling	0.0	2.3	2.3
Some Primary (1–4 years of schooling)	0.2	3.8	4.0
Primary (5–9)	0.9	16.6	17.5
Secondary (10–14)	10.2	52.8	63.0
College Graduate or Higher	42.2	46.8	89.0
By Social Group			
Scheduled Tribes	4.3	15.5	19.8
Scheduled Caste	3.4	17.8	21.2
Other Backward Castes	5.2	21.9	27.1
General	10.7	28.5	39.2
By Geography			
Urban	12.4	30.2	42.6
Rural	3.2	18.4	21.6

Source: Data has been tabulated using the India Human Development Survey Round 2 published in 2015.

schooling, 17.5% for those with primary schooling constituting five to nine years, and virtually zero for those with lesser years of schooling. This positive relationship between English-speaking ability and educational attainment is understandable given that English is not the native language for the majority of the Indian population, where the foremost introduction to language stems from school exposure. Most non-native English speakers are exposed to English language in middle schools, thereby establishing a positive relationship between educational attainment and English-speaking capabilities.

English-speaking ability also varies according to the social groups in India. The two most disadvantaged social groups are the Scheduled Tribes (STs) and Scheduled Castes (SCs). The Other Backward Castes (OBCs), though at a better ritual standing than the SCs, are also much worse off than the

Higher Castes. English-speaking proficiency is greater amongst the higher castes relative to the disadvantaged social groups. Various socio-economic factors can explain this difference, including low educational attainment and relatively lower incomes amongst the disadvantaged groups, as well as the geographical isolation of the Scheduled Tribes and the rural concentration of the Scheduled Castes.

Finally, there exists a large variation in English ability by geographical status categorised into urban and rural, with the former comprising almost double the number of English speakers relative to the latter. Forty-two point six percent of people living in urban areas can speak English as compared to 21.6% of individuals in rural areas. The distribution of English ability across states in provided in Table 3.2. Evidently, English abilities differ tremendously across states. While Chhattisgarh represents the least number of English speakers (17.7%), Manipur represents the highest number of English speakers (89.9%).

While it is beyond the scope of this book to account for all the cross-state differences (though the book will address the relationship between the growth of and English ability in the states), it is interesting to see the change in English-speaking abilities across states relative to the 2005 figures. Twenty-four out of the 33 states for which data is available saw an increase in English speakers from 2005. While this increase is consistent with the fact that, overall, India has seen an increase in the number of English speakers over the years, the degree of change between 2005 and 2011 for some states reflects a prominent limitation of the dataset. Just like most household surveys, IHDS's limitation is that it presents data of the *perception* of English ability, since the answers are based on the interviewees' own opinions of their English capability rather than a tested methodology. Nevertheless, it is the only large-scale individual-level dataset in India that contains a measure of English language skills, and it is therefore helpful for this study. However, readers must keep in mind that the findings of this chapter are based on the *perception* of English ability.

English language and hourly wages in India

In India, the raw difference in earnings between people who speak English and people who do not is large. . . . After controlling for age, social group, schooling, geography and proxies for ability, we find that there are large, statistically significant returns to English language skills in India.

– (Mehtabul Azam, Aimee Chin, and Nishith Prakash, 2011)

It is common wisdom that English language skills in India are valuable. However, this benefit of higher returns had not been quantified for the longest

Table 3.2 Percentage of English speakers distributed by states

State ID	*State*	*Percentage of Indians with Fluent English Ability in 2011 (1)*	*Percentage of Indians with Little English Ability in 2011 (2)*	*Percentage of Indians with No English Ability in 2011 (3)*	*Total Percentage of Indians with English Ability in 2011 (4) = (1)+(2)*	*Total Percentage of Indian with English Ability in 2005 (5)*	*Change in English-speaking Ability Over the Years (6) = (4)–(5)*
1.	Jammu and Kashmir	10.7	36.2	53.1	**46.9**	35.3	**11.6**
2.	Himachal Pradesh	6.4	28.7	64.9	**35.1**	37.2	**–2.1**
3.	Punjab	5.2	36.7	58.1	**41.9**	54.8	**–12.9**
4.	Chandigarh	22.3	52.4	25.3	**74.7**	79.3	**–4.6**
5.	Uttarakhand	5.4	27.0	67.6	**32.4**	30.0	**2.4**
6.	Haryana	8.3	32.0	59.7	**40.3**	22.3	**18**
7.	Delhi	14.5	34.6	50.9	**49.1**	41.6	**7.5**
8.	Rajasthan	6.5	18.2	75.3	**24.7**	16.5	**8.2**
9.	Uttar Pradesh	2.7	18.2	79.1	**20.9**	18.9	**2**
10.	Bihar	4.9	19.4	75.7	**24.4**	13.8	**10.6**
11.	Sikkim	18.0	31.0	51.0	**49.0**	53.5	**–4.5**
12.	Arunachal Pradesh	16.0	30.8	53.2	**46.8**	58.5	**–11.7**
13.	Nagaland	41.1	40.7	18.2	**81.8**	79.6	**2.2**
14.	Manipur	42.7	47.2	10.1	**89.9**	64.3	**25.6**
15.	Mizoram	18.9	37.5	43.6	**56.4**	81.2	**–24.8**
16.	Tripura	1.7	18.1	80.2	**19.8**	6.2	**13.6**
17.	Meghalaya	22.3	35.4	42.3	**57.7**	56.2	**1.5**
18.	Assam	4.2	16.2	79.6	**20.4**	30.9	**–10.5**
19.	West Bengal	4.3	15.5	80.2	**19.8**	13.4	**6.4**
20.	Jharkhand	5.8	25.0	69.2	**30.8**	11.0	**19.8**
21.	Orissa	6.2	19.6	74.2	**25.8**	9.5	**16.3**
22.	Chhattisgarh	2.3	15.4	82.3	**17.7**	8.2	**9.5**
23.	Madhya Pradesh	1.9	16.7	81.4	**18.6**	8.6	**10**
24.	Gujarat	5.3	17.9	76.8	**23.2**	13.0	**10.2**

(*Continued*)

Table 3.2 (Continued)

State ID	*State*	*Percentage of Indians with Fluent English Ability in 2011 (1)*	*Percentage of Indians with Little English Ability in 2011 (2)*	*Percentage of Indians with No English Ability in 2011 (3)*	*Total Percentage of Indians with English Ability in 2011 (4) = (1)+(2)*	*Total Percentage of Indian with English Ability in 2005 (5)*	*Change in English-speaking Ability Over the Years (6) = (4)–(5)*
25.	Daman and Diu	8.4	27.2	64.4	**35.6**	17.3	**18.3**
26.	Dadra and Nagar Haveli	13.9	33.5	52.6	**47.4**	24.8	**22.6**
27.	Maharashtra	8.8	24.3	66.9	**33.1**	23.6	**9.5**
28.	Andhra Pradesh (including Telangana)	5.7	24.8	69.5	**30.5**	15.6	**14.9**
29.	Karnataka	6.2	19.6	74.2	**25.8**	18.4	7.4
30.	Goa	16.1	35.4	48.5	**51.5**	83.8	**–32.3**
31.	Lakshadweep	n/a	n/a	n/a	**n/a**	n/a	**n/a**
32.	Kerala	13.2	40.7	46.1	**53.9**	32.3	**21.6**
33.	Tamil Nadu	11.4	28.3	60.3	**39.7**	26.9	**12.8**
34.	Pondicherry	19.1	21.5	59.4	**40.6**	55.0	**–14.4**
35.	Andaman and Nicobar	n/a	n/a	n/a	**n/a**	n/a	**n/a**

Source: The data for the year 2011 has been tabulated using the India Human Development Survey Round 2 published in 2015. The data for the year 2005 has been tabulated using the India Human Development Survey Round 1. The categorisation of the 2005 figures into fluent speakers and partial speakers is provided in Appendix 3.

Note: IHDS Rounds 1 and 2 did not contain data for Lakshadweep and Andaman and Nicobar Islands, given the small population of these union territories. The data for Telangana is included in that for Andhra Pradesh since the former did not become a separate state until 2014, while the data was collected in 2011.

time due to lack of data. Finally, in 2011, the first and only nationally representative quantification was presented by Azam, Chin and Prakash, who utilised the then recently published 2005 IHDS Round 1 dataset that contained measures of English-speaking ability and earnings. I would urge the readers to see Azam, Chin and Prakash's seminal work, which thoroughly quantifies the returns to the English language in India.

Similar estimation, however, could not be done consistently in the following years, since IHDS did not conduct a second survey until 2011, which only became available in 2015. The recent availability of IHDS Round 2 enables me to quantify the latest returns to English skills.

Similar to Azam, Chin and Prakash, I approximate the relationship between English language skills and earnings using the following equation:

$$Earnings_i = \propto + \beta English_i + \pi X_i + \varepsilon_i \quad (1)$$

whereby $Earnings_i$ is the log of hourly earnings of individual i, $English_i$ is the measure of English language skills of individual i, and X_i is the set of demographic characters including age, age squared,[23] social group and gender. The coefficient of interest is β, which will give us the estimate of the impact of English language skills on the log of earnings.[24]

The equation presented previously is, however, a simplistic one, as there are other relevant variables that determine earnings. If these variables are not considered, the estimation of the coefficient of interest, β, will face an upward bias due to omitted variable bias. It is therefore necessary to include certain variables, suggested by Azam, Chin and Prakash in their 2005 estimation model. These variables include years of schooling, geography and proxies for ability.

Due to the predominant implementation of the Three-Language Formula, early grades of schooling usually use the native language as the medium of instruction. Even in schools that promote English language teaching from the start, the chances of students being familiar with the language are low since 99.8% of the population have alternative native languages that they are accustomed to using at home, and ergo are fluent in. It is usually in later grades that the children get accustomed to the English language, thereby reflecting a positive correlation between years of schooling and English proficiency. This positive relationship between the two variables can lead to the OLS estimate of β to be an upward bias. To avoid this, I incorporate years of schooling in the equation to control for it.

People with higher ability are more likely to have better English skills as well as better job returns. It is therefore important to control for ability. Controlling for years of schooling does partially reduce the ability bias because people with greater ability are likely to complete more years of schooling. However, this control is imperfect, since incorporation of other variables is required. Azam, Chin, and Prakash (2011) used individuals' responses to secondary school leaving certification (SSLC) examination performance and whether they had failed or repeated a year as the proxies for ability in their paper. SSLC is a certification obtained by students of India after successfully completing an examination at the end of 10th grade (secondary school level). A SSLC makes one eligible for further education, and better SSLC performance enables one to attend good schools. The scholars conceded that, while SSLC exam performance is a credible proxy for ability in the Indian context, the information is only available for individuals who have completed 10th grade. This constitutes only 30% of their IHDS Round 1 working age sample. Due to this limitation, they propagated using individuals' responses to whether they have failed or repeated a year as the second measure for ability to incorporate those with limited years of schooling. Adapting from Azam, Chin and Prakash, I use both SSLC exam performance and responses to repeated/failed year as my measures for ability.

Finally, English is more prevalent in major cities. However, these major cities also have relatively higher wages. In order to control for the effects that geographical characteristics have on wages, so as to get a more accurate estimation of the impact of English proficiency on earnings, I control for urban residence and state of residence. To control for geographic characteristics more finely so as to obtain intra-district (rather than inter-district) variation, I include district of residence fixed effects. This will enable us to compare individuals who speak English and those who do not speak English *within* the same district.

Given the relevance of the discussed variables, I modify Equation 1 as follows:

$$Earnings_i = \propto_r + \beta English_i + \gamma Schooling_i + \delta Ability_i + \varphi Urban_i + \pi X_i + \varepsilon_i \qquad (2)$$

where $\propto_r$ is the state or district fixed effect, $Schooling_i$ is years of schooling completed by individual i, $Ability_i$ is the proxy for ability (including SSLC exam performance and failing or repeating a grade) and $Urban_i$ is whether individual i lives in an urban area. The rationale for using an earning estimation equation similar to Azam, Chin and Prakash's is to enable a comparison between the effects of English language on earning in 2011 to that in 2005. The descriptive statistics for the independent variables that will be used in the regression is presented in Appendix 4.

Since we need to estimate earnings, I take the log of the response to hourly wages and bonuses in the previous year as the independent variable in the regression. Using the sample of both male and female wage earners aged 18 to 65, I estimate Equation 2 using the ordinary least squares estimation method. The results are reported in Table 3.3, with each column adding the aforementioned controls.

Column 1 reports the difference in log hourly wages due to English ability without any controls. Compared to individuals with no English skills,

Table 3.3 Effect of English speaking ability on log hourly wages

	No Controls (1)	*Demographic Controls (2)*	*Education Controls (3)*	*Geographic Controls (4)*	*Ability Controls (5)*	*District Fixed Effects (6)*
Fluent English	1.158***	1.034***	0.529***	0.474***	0.440***	**0.338*** **
	(0.0195)	(0.0192)	(0.0241)	(0.0236)	(0.0237)	**(0.0229)**
Little English	0.453***	0.357***	0.128***	0.111***	0.110***	**0.072*** **
	(0.0113)	(0.0112)	(0.0125)	(0.0120)	(0.0126)	**(0.0114)**
Age		0.008***	0.010***	0.009***	0.012***	0.009***
		(0.0007)	(0.0007)	(0.0007)	(0.0009)	(0.0008)
Age^2		–0.007**	–0.006**	–0.006*	0.003	0.006*
		(0.0023)	(0.0031)	(0.0030)	(0.0039)	(0.0036)
Gender: Female		–0.428***	–0.380***	–0.374***	–0.361***	–0.370***
		(0.0078)	(0.0079)	(0.0079)	(0.0112)	(0.0111)
Caste: Other Backward Castes (OBC)		–0.129***	–0.076***	–0.065***	–0.076***	–0.046***
		(0.0104)	(0.0103)	(0.0099)	(0.0116)	(0.0119)
Caste: Scheduled Castes (SC)		–0.149***	–0.068***	–0.048***	–0.041***	–0.033***
		(0.0114)	(0.0112)	(0.0109)	(0.0132)	(0.0130)
Caste: Scheduled Tribes (ST)		–0.309***	–0.220***	–0.165***	–0.135***	–0.058***
		(0.0135)	(0.0133)	(0.0130)	(0.0175)	(0.0183)
Caste: Other Castes		0.046	0.067**	0.088***	0.100**	0.047
		(0.0370)	(0.0333)	(0.0357)	(0.0439)	(0.0434)
Religion: Muslim		–0.111***	–0.051***	–0.077***	–0.055***	–0.059***
		(0.0120)	(0.0120)	(0.0118)	(0.0152)	(0.0154)
Religion: Christian		0.373***	0.353***	0.323***	0.316***	0.061**
		(0.0240)	(0.0235)	(0.0233)	(0.0256)	(0.0272)
Religion: Sikh		0.036	0.035	0.056	0.020	0.072
		(0.0407)	(0.0416)	(0.0409)	(0.0532)	(0.0514)
Religion: Buddhist		–0.035	–0.058*	–0.060*	–0.040	0.012
		(0.0340)	(0.0351)	(0.0329)	(0.0349)	(0.0353)

(Continued)

Table 3.3 (Continued)

	No Controls (1)	*Demographic Controls (2)*	*Education Controls (3)*	*Geographic Controls (4)*	*Ability Controls (5)*	*District Fixed Effects (6)*
Religion: Jain		0.058	0.074	0.032	0.144	0.196**
		(0.0991)	(0.0892)	(0.0846)	(0.1069)	(0.0940)
Religion: Tribal		0.026	0.072**	0.087**	0.077*	0.000
		(0.0396)	(0.0365)	(0.0355)	(0.0447)	(0.0545)
Religion: Others		0.129**	0.109**	0.114**	0.126*	–0.032
		(0.0555)	(0.0493)	(0.0521)	(0.0671)	(0.0721)
Religion: None		0.687***	0.853***	0.840***	0.810***	0.517
		(0.2061)	(0.2539)	(0.3046)	(0.3010)	(0.4708)
Years of Schooling Completed: 1			–0.035	–0.050	–0.100*	0.160
			(0.0441)	(0.0422)	(0.0587)	(0.0533)
Years of Schooling Completed: 2			0.033*	0.017	–0.017	0.0170
			(0.0199)	(0.0195)	(0.0433)	(0.0401)
Years of Schooling Completed: 3			0.015	–0.008	–0.037	–0.002
			(0.0178)	(0.0173)	(0.0425)	(0.0395)
Years of Schooling Completed: 4			0.078***	0.056***	0.025	0.050
			(0.0167)	(0.0162)	(0.0418)	(0.0388)
Years of Schooling Completed: 5			0.115***	0.088***	0.066	0.072*
(Primary School Completion)			(0.0136)	(0.0133)	(0.0407)	(0.0378)
Years of Schooling Completed: 6			0.158***	0.110***	0.101**	0.083**
			(0.0193)	(0.0189)	(0.0430)	(0.0398)
Years of Schooling Completed: 7			0.166***	0.126***	0.115***	0.098***
			(0.0149)	(0.0147)	(0.0411)	(0.0384)
Years of Schooling Completed: 8			0.154***	0.111***	0.113***	0.122***
(Middle School Completion)			(0.0173)	(0.0169)	(0.0411)	(0.0380)
Years of Schooling Completed: 9			0.189***	0.143***	0.148***	0.123***
			(0.0141)	(0.0138)	(0.0409)	(0.0381)

Years of Schooling Completed: 10 (Secondary School Completion)			0.329***	0.260***	0.288***	0.197***
			(0.0157)	(0.0154)	(0.0548)	(0.0514)
Years of Schooling Completed: 11			0.152***	0.108***	0.155***	0.163***
			(0.0290)	(0.0278)	(0.0606)	(0.0567)
Years of Schooling Completed: 12 (Higher Secondary School Completion)			0.371***	0.304***	0.332***	0.264***
			(0.0207)	(0.0201)	((0.0575)	(0.0537)
Years of Schooling Completed: 13			0.442***	0.345***	0.376***	0.333***
			(0.0556)	(0.0539)	(0.0765)	(0.0716)
Years of Schooling Completed: 14			0.399***	0.320***	0.349***	0.288***
			(0.0542)	(0.0526)	(0.0754)	(0.0701)
Years of Schooling Completed: 15 (Bachelor's Degree)			0.676***	0.575***	0.568***	0.486***
			(0.0244)	(0.0244)	(0.0597)	(0.0560)
Years of Schooling Completed: 16 (Above Bachelor's Degree)			0.871***	0.784***	0.759***	0.753***
			(0.0336)	(0.0331)	(0.0635)	(0.0600)
Urban Residence				0.268***	0.273***	0.186***
				(0.0083)	(0.0099)	(0.0126)
SSLC Exam Performance: Class I					0.103**	0.104***
					(0.0444)	(0.0420)
SSLC Exam Performance: Class II					–0.057	–0.005
					(0.0401)	(0.0379)
SSLC Exam Performance: Class III					–0.071*	–0.066*
					(0.0415)	(0.0392)
Has Repeated/Failed a Grade					–0.036***	–0.040***
					(0.0109)	(0.0103)
R-Squared	0.174	0.275	0.315	0.339	0.330	0.432

Notes: The sample consists of individuals, both male and female, aged 18–65 who reported wage and salary work (34,335 observations in Column 6, with all the comprehensive controls) in India Human Development Survey-Round 2 (2011). The omitted caste group is Higher Caste. The omitted religion dummy is Hindu. The omitted educational attainment group is zero years of schooling completed. The omitted dummy for SSLC exam performance is those who reported valid blank i.e. did not give the SSLC exam (there were a few values not pertaining to any sub-category that needed to be cleaned or dropped). Asterisk denotes significance level (= 10%, ** = 5% and *** = 1%). Robust Standard Errors are shown in parentheses.*

individuals with fluent skills earn 1.158 log points more and individuals with little skills earn 0.543 log points more. These differences are, however, overstated, since English skills are related to other indicators that affect earnings.

Column 2 considers one such indicator – demography. Accounting for demographic factors including age, gender, caste and religion reduces the impact of English skills on earnings. Controlling for education in Column 3 by adding the dummies for years of schooling further reduces the estimation of β, and greatly so (by more than half). Adding geographic controls in Column 4, by including a dummy for urban residence, helps control for labour market institution. In Column 5, I add SSLC exam performance and grade failure/repetition to control for ability, and finally, in Column 6, I include state and district fixed effects to get a more detailed geographic control.

The specification presented in Column 6 has comprehensive controls, thereby making the estimation relatively more accurate. The model is also one with the best fit, reflected by the highest R-Square (in the last row of Table 3.3). While a few dummies of the independent variables were not significant, overall each independent variable was highly significant at 1% significance level. To check for heteroskedasticity (in order to have constant variance), I used robust standard errors. The multicollinearity did not exist in the final model, as the variation inflation factor (vif) was low for English as well as the overall model.

The estimates in Column 6 highlight that, relative to individuals with no English-speaking ability in the IHDS Round 2 sample of wage earners, individuals with fluent English-speaking ability earn approximately 34% more, while individuals with little English-speaking skills earn approximately 7% more.

These estimates are not only large but also statistically significant and constitute as undoubtedly meaningful economic effects. The degree of the economic effects of these results is substantiated by the fact that the returns to fluent English-speaking ability are higher than the returns to a Class I qualification in SSLC exam, higher-secondary education, as well as being an urban resident. In other words, fluent English-speaking ability garners a higher wage relative to a high school degree or a Class I qualification in SSLC.[25]

Since Azam, Chin and Prakash found the returns to English in 2005 separately for men and women, I do the same for the 2011 data to enable comparison. The estimation yields the following results.

We again see that English-speaking ability has statistically significant and high returns for men (Table 3.4, Column 1). Men with fluent English ability earn 31.5% more and men with little English ability earn 6% more than men with no English ability. The returns to English ability are again greater than the returns to higher secondary education. Azam, Chin and Prakash's estimation using the IHDS Round 1 for 2005 yielded that men with fluent English skills earned 34% more than men with no English skills, while men with little English skills earned 13% more. The 3.5% difference in the returns to fluent English ability between 2005 and 2011 does not necessarily imply a reduction in the returns to English over time. It can indeed be explained by the mild differences in estimation methodologies and changes in sample[26] in the two studies. For instance, I included religion, a statistically significant variable in the earnings regression for men, as a demographic control since IHDS Round 2 provided me with the option to do so. IHDS Round 1, on the other hand, had an accumulated variable for caste and religion, in which various dummies were missing. Due to this data limitation, Azam, Chin and Prakash's estimation did not take into account all religions as a demographic control, thereby yielding a relatively overstated estimation. Since the controls in this study are comparatively more comprehensive, my estimation of the effects of fluent English ability on earnings is understandably lower.

My estimation of the returns to little English ability on earnings for men is however nearly half that of Azam, Chin and Prakash's study. While alterations in estimation methodology, sampling and controls account for this reduced approximation to an extent, it would be reasonable to infer that the returns to little English skills for men have reduced, since fluency is the supreme job requirement.

Furthermore, the results show that women who converse fluently in English earn 41.6% more relative to women with no English-speaking ability, and women who converse little in English earn 12.3% more (Table 3.4, Column 2).

On running the regression, however, I found that religion (as a demographic control) and the response to failed/repeated year (a proxy for ability) were insignificant when estimating the returns for women.[27] Upon dropping these variables, I obtained coefficients of approximately 40% for women with fluent English ability and 10% for women with little English ability (Table 3.4, Column 3). The drawback of estimating the returns to English without inclusion of failed/repeated year is that, though it increased the number of observations, it weakened the ability proxy, thereby weakening the fit of the model (R-Square = 0.396). Furthermore, the vif of the model was as high as 7.47, suggesting higher degree of multicollinearity amongst the independent variables.

Finally, I ran a regression keeping responses for failed/repeated years in the equation, while eliminating religion. This equation is the closest to that of Azam, Chin, and Prakash's (2011), who did not include religion as a separate independent variable due to IHDS Round 1 data limitation. As evident in Table 3.4, Column 4, this methodology reported coefficients of 41.8% for women with fluent English-speaking ability and 12.5% for women with little English-speaking ability.

Though Column 4 of Table 3.4 is my preferred specification for the returns to English ability for women, the results are still imprecise. This is because selective participation in wage-employment is a much more serious problem for women relative to men. Only approximately 41% of the working- age sample in IHDS Round 2 reported earning wages and salaries. Out of these, only 30% were women, while the remaining 70% were men. With

Table 3.4 Effect of English speaking ability on log hourly wages

	Men *(1)*	*Women* *(2)*	*Women (without Religion and Failed/Repeated Year Controls)* *(3)*	*Women (without Religion Control)* *(4)*
English-Speaking Ability				
Fluent English	**0.315***** **(0.0248)**	0.416*** (0.0576)	0.402*** (0.0564)	**0.418***** **(0.0577)**
Little English	**0.060***** **(0.0121)**	0.123*** (0.0325)	0.098*** (0.0275)	**0.125***** **(0.0325)**
Age	0.009*** (0.0009)	0.014*** (0.002)	0.007*** (0.0011)	0.014*** (0.0020)
Age^2	0.007* (0.0040)	0.000 (0.0086)	–0.007 (0.0045)	–0.001 (0.0086)
Caste				
Other Backward Castes (OBC)	–0.056*** (0.0128)	0.011 (0.0308)	0.028 (0.0220)	0.010 (0.0308)
Scheduled Castes (SC)	–0.048*** (0.0142)	0.053 (0.0332)	0.046** (0.0228)	0.063* (0.0327)
Scheduled Tribes (ST)	–0.087*** (0.0201)	0.055 (0.0441)	0.038 (0.0257)	0.064 (0.0436)
Other Castes	0.019 (0.0495)	0.169* (0.0903)	0.071 (0.0559)	0.165* (0.0907)
Religion				
Muslim	–0.063*** (0.0158)	–0.076 (0.0481)		
Christian	0.063** (0.0306)	0.052 (0.0549)		
Sikh	0.061 (0.0567)	0.155 (0.1116)		
Buddhist	–0.009 (0.0406)	0.033 (0.0670)		

Jain	0.276***	–0.378		
	(0.1011)	(0.2346)		
Tribal	0.006	–0.024		
	(0.0614)	(0.0999)		
Others	–0.017	–0.204		
	(0.0790)	(0.1351)		
None	0.747	–0.012		
	(0.5728)	(0.4663)		
Years of Schooling				
Years of Schooling Completed: 1	0.034	–0.078	–0.068	–0.077
	(0.0577)	(0.1155)	(0.0804)	(0.1161)
Years of Schooling Completed: 2	–0.015	0.088	0.041	0.088
	(0.0447)	(0.0809)	(0.0327)	(0.0817)
Years of Schooling Completed: 3	0.003	–0.002	–0.043	0.002
	(0.0441)	(0.0785)	(0.0286)	(0.0795)
Years of Schooling Completed: 4	0.028	0.098	0.053**	0.101
	(0.0434)	(0.0769)	(0.0267)	(0.0778)
Years of Schooling Completed: 5	0.052	0.130*	0.059***	0.131*
(Primary School Completion)	(0.0418)	(0.0756)	(0.0232)	(0.0765)
Years of Schooling Completed: 6	0.067	0.118	0.032	0.122
	(0.0439)	(0.0845)	(0.0397)	(0.0853)
Years of Schooling Completed: 7	0.094**	0.108	0.027	0.113
	(0.0423)	(0.0778)	(0.0273)	(0.0787)
Years of Schooling Completed: 8	0.105***	0.162*	0.071**	0.168*
(Middle School Completion)	(0.0417)	(0.0794)	(0.0307)	(0.0802)
Years of Schooling Completed: 9	0.096**	0.223***	0.108***	0.227***
	(0.0421)	(0.0789)	(0.0302)	(0.0796)
Years of Schooling Completed: 10 (Secondary School	0.187***	0.220**	0.130	0.228**
Completion)	(0.0571)	(0.1114)	(0.0858)	(0.1124)
Years of Schooling Completed: 11	0.131**	0.322***	0.219**	0.331***
	(0.0624)	(0.1291)	(0.1075)	(0.1298)
Years of Schooling Completed: 12	0.228***	0.419***	0.335***	0.428***
(Higher Secondary School Completion)	(0.0595)	(0.1197)	(0.0965)	(0.1201)

(Continued)

Table 3.4 (Continued)

	Men (1)	*Women (2)*	*Women (without Religion and Failed/Repeated Year Controls) (3)*	*Women (without Religion Control) (4)*
Years of Schooling Completed: 13	0.332***	0.401***	0.282**	0.418***
	(0.0835)	(0.1387)	(0.1183)	(0.1391)
Years of Schooling Completed: 14	0.233***	0.443***	0.332***	0.454***
	(0.0797)	(0.1469)	(0.1315)	(0.1479)
Years of Schooling Completed: 15	0.459***	0.655***	0.585***	0.666***
(Bachelor's Degree)	(0.0622)	(0.1249)	(0.1037)	(0.1254)
Years of Schooling Completed: 16	0.693***	0.983***	0.940***	0.994***
(Above Bachelor's Degree)	(0.0671)	(0.1291)	(0.1084)	(0.1296)
Urban Residence	0.185***	0.142***	0.117***	0.137***
	(0.0135)	(0.0330)	(0.0220)	(0.0328)
SSLC Exam Performance				
Class I	0.090**	0.125	0.109	0.123
	(0.0472)	(0.0931)	(0.0943)	(0.0936)
Class II	−0.007	0.016	0.004	0.014
	(0.0422)	(0.0888)	(0.0899)	(0.0891)
Class III	−0.057	−0.097	−0.097	−0.098
	(0.0436)	(0.0924)	(0.0938)	(0.0926)
Has Repeated/ Failed a Grade	−0.038***	−0.021		−0.023
	(0.0112)	(0.0246)		(0.0245)
District Fixed Effects	Yes	Yes	Yes	Yes
R-Squared	0.416	0.468	0.396	0.467
Observations	27,262	7,073	15,318	7.073

Notes: The sample consists of individuals, both male and female, aged 18–65 who reported wage and salary work in India Human Development Survey-Round 2 (2011). The genders are, however, segregated for the analysis. The omitted caste group is Higher Caste. The omitted religion dummy is Hindu. The omitted educational attainment group is zero years of schooling completed. The omitted dummy for SSLC exam performance is those who reported valid blank i.e. did not give the SSLC exam (there were a few values not pertaining to any sub-category that needed to be cleaned or dropped). Asterisk denotes significance level (= 10%, ** = 5% and *** = 1%). Robust Standard Errors are shown in parentheses.*

all the demographic, educational and ability controls in place, the overall observations for working-age individuals in wage employment drops further. From this limited sample of the working age population participating in wage employment, 79% were men and only 21% were women. This selective participation can lead to biased estimates for women due to non-random sampling. Even Azam, Chin and Prakash faced a similar problem while estimating the returns for English ability for women in 2005.

Nevertheless, taking into consideration that the results might be imprecise, I still found a positive relationship between English ability and earnings ranging between 40% to 42% higher earnings for women with fluent English ability relative to those with no English ability, and 10% to 12% higher earnings for women with little English ability. Azam, Chin and Prakash had estimated the earnings of women fluent in English as 22% more than those with no English-speaking ability. For women with little English-speaking ability, their approximation was 10%. Since the methodology of estimation between the two papers was very similar, it is reasonable to infer that the returns to fluent English for women have almost doubled in a few years. It is also noteworthy that the returns to English ability in wage-employment are higher for women (approximately 40–42%) than for men (approximately 32%). A possible explanation for this difference could be that women in wage-employment primarily belong to the service sector, while men in wage-employment belong to both manufacturing and service sectors. As discussed in the previous section of this book, service sector wages are perhaps more sensitive to English ability than manufacturing sector wages. This point will be substantiated empirically in the following sections of this chapter.

Overall, one can conclude that there are positive, high and statistically significant returns to English-speaking ability in India. Individuals who know fluent English earn 33.8% more than individuals who have no English-speaking ability, and individuals who possess little English-speaking ability earn 7.2% more than those with no English-speaking ability. Amongst these, men who can converse fluently earn 31.5% more than those who speak no English. Men who speak little English earn 6% more. On the other hand, women who speak fluent English earn 41.8% more than those with no English-speaking ability. Women who speak little English earn 12.5% more. Therefore, the English language is positively correlated to earnings in wage-employment in India.

English language and household income in India

[Selection bias] could be serious in the context of India, where over 70% of the population is rural, and family farms and non-farm businesses continue to absorb much of the labour force.

– (Mehtabul Azam, Aimee Chin, and Nishith Prakash, 2011)

Estimating the effects of the English language on hourly wages faces a selection bias – it only accounts for those people who report earning wages. It is widely accepted that individuals who speak English in India are more likely to be in wage employment, thereby imbedding the bias. Moreover, a large part of the Indian population belongs to farm and non-farm businesses, who might not necessarily speak English and yet earn a reasonable income. This implies that the previous estimation might have a bias due to selective sampling of those people who are in jobs that have higher returns to English. To correct this, there is a need to make the sample less selective and more random.

The remedy for offsetting the section bias was provided by Azam, Chin and Prakash in their 2011 paper. They prescribed the usage of Household Income and Household Consumption as the dependent variables, instead of hourly wages. The rationale behind using household income and household consumption is that these are measures of earnings that are observed regardless of an individual's employment status. The analysis with the household income and consumption measures must also be done using household heads so as to avoid counting the same household multiple times. The results yielded with these changed dependent variables are provided in Table 3.5.

As evident from Table 3.5, Column 1, household heads in wage employment who speak fluent English earn 37.5% more than household heads in wage employment who speak no English. This is approximately 3% higher than the returns we observed for all household members who speak English

Table 3.5 Returns to English-speaking skills – household heads (2011)

	Household Head's Log Hourly Wages (1)	*Household's Log Per Capita Income Last Year (2)*	*Household's Log Per Capita Expenditure Last Year (3)*
Fluent English	0.375***	0.328***	0.228***
	(0.0362)	(0.0364)	(0.0224)
Little English	0.076***	0.073***	0.082***
	(0.0178)	(0.0203)	(0.0124)
District Fixed Effects	Yes	Yes	Yes
R-Squared	0.447	0.366	0.417
Observations	15,196	25,013	25,319

Notes: The sample consists of individuals, both male and female, aged 18–65 who reported as being household heads.in India Human Development Survey-Round 2 (2011). For controls, the omitted caste group is Higher Caste. The omitted religion dummy is Hindu. The omitted educational attainment group is zero years of schooling completed. The omitted dummy for SSLC exam performance is those who reported valid blank i.e. did not give the SSLC exam (there were a few values not pertaining to any sub-category that needed to be cleaned or dropped). Asterisk denotes significance level (= 10%, ** = 5%and *** = 1%). Robust Standard Errors are shown in parentheses.*

fluently. This difference could be attributed to the fact that household heads in general are more experienced with more years of employment. Household heads with little English-speaking skills earn 7.6% more than household heads with no English-speaking ability. This is consistent with the returns to little English-speaking ability I estimated for all members of the household reported in Table 3.3.

Upon analysing the effects of English ability on household per capita income (Table 3.5, Column 2), we see that a household with a fluent English-speaking household head has 32.8% more per capita income than a household where the head speaks no English. A household where the head speaks little English earns 7.3% more per capita income than a household where the head does not speak English. Here, we have accounted for all households, regardless of the whether the head is in wage employment, farm business or non-farm business. Since the heads of households are not circumscribed to wage employment – an area in which English speakers are more likely to participate – there is no selective sampling bias. By correcting the bias, we see that the estimates of English ability on per capita income are consistent with the estimate we got in Column 6 of Table 3.3. Therefore, there are statistically significant returns of approximately 32.8–33.8% to fluent English ability and approximately 7% to little English ability in India.

The high and significant impact of English is also visible on per capita expenditure. Households where the head speaks fluent English have 22.8% higher per capita expenditures than households where the head speaks no English. This positive implication of English on per capita expenditure is also observed in households where the heads speak little English. In such households, the effect of English is 8.2% higher relative to households with a non-English-speaking head.

Segregation of household heads by gender highlights that 92% of our household heads are men. Since household heads in our observation are predominantly men, the findings on the impact of English on household earnings and consumption are not applicable to women. Limiting the sample of household heads to only men yields the results reported in Table 3.6. These findings of the impact of English on the wages, household income and consumption for male household heads are consistent with those observed in Table 3.5. Therefore, while I have corrected for the non-random sampling bias for the estimates on the returns to English for men, the bias cannot be corrected for women.

Returns to the English language by sectors

An effect on earnings is more likely to occur in the sectors that depend on English for conducting business, which would include multi-national companies, exporters and importers

Table 3.6 Returns to English-speaking skills – male household heads (2011)

	Household Head's Log Hourly Wages	*Household's Log Total Income of the Previous Year*	*Household's Log Per Capita Expenditure*
Fluent English	0.372***	0.272***	0.221***
	(0.0367)	(0.0361)	(0.0230)
Little English	0.069***	0.060***	0.082***
	(0.0178)	(0.0215)	(0.0128)
District Fixed Effects	Yes	Yes	Yes
R-Squared	0.448	0.346	0.426
Observations	14,508	22,983	23,268

Notes: The sample consists of males aged 18–65 who reported as being household heads in India Human Development Survey-Round 2 (2011). For controls, the omitted caste group is Higher Caste. The omitted religion dummy is Hindu. The omitted educational attainment group is zero years of schooling completed. The omitted dummy for SSLC exam performance is those who reported valid blank i.e. did not give the SSLC exam (there were a few values not pertaining to any sub-category that needed to be cleaned or dropped). Asterisk denotes significance level (= 10%, ** = 5% and *** = 1%). Robust Standard Errors are shown in parenthesis.*

> *who have links to global markets, and service sector businesses. In the case of the latter, communication is a core part of business, and value is produced through language-related activity including advertising, marketing, promoting, receiving guests and clients, and servicing.*
>
> – (Philip Powell-Davies, 2015)[28]

In the theoretical conceptualisation of the language-growth relationship, I had stated that the language has significant economic effects in a developing country like India (relative to a non-English dependent, yet high growth developing country like China) because India has a service-driven economy. From interviews, I was able to gather that the economic impacts of English are greater in the service sector than in the manufacturing sector. By extension, the returns to English-speaking ability must be higher in the service sector than in the manufacturing and agricultural sectors. In order to substantiate this, I estimate a modified version of Equation 2 separately for individuals belonging to the primary/agricultural sector, secondary/manufacturing sector and tertiary/service sector.

In Equation 2, I had added demographic controls, educational controls, ability controls and geographical controls. In order to investigate the returns to English language separately for the three sectors, it is also necessary to add occupational controls in the equation. This is because within each sector, some occupations earn higher than the others. For instance, in the service sector, a client-facing manager at a firm will earn more than an analyst in the same firm. To account for these earning differences caused by occupation, it is important to control for it and modify Equation 2 as follows:

$$Earnings_i = \propto_r + \beta English_i + \gamma Schooling_i + \delta Ability_i + \varphi Urban_i + \sigma Occupation_i + \pi X_i + \varepsilon_i \quad (3)$$

where $\propto_r$ is the district fixed effects, $Schooling_i$ is years of schooling completed by individual *i*, $Ability_i$ is the proxy for ability (including SSLC exam performance and failing or repeating a grade), $Urban_i$ is whether individual *i* lives in an urban area, $Occupation_i$ is the occupation of individuals *i* within the sector, and X_i are demographic variables including age, age-square, gender, religion and caste.

I preliminarily segregate the entire working age sample of IHDS Round 2 into the three sectors – agricultural/primary, manufacturing/secondary and service/tertiary. This categorisation was possible since IHDS Round 2 extensively incorporated responses to the industry everyone belonged to.

I then take wages/salaries as the proxy for earnings in Equation 3 and use the equation to estimate the effects of the English language on those individuals who reported as earning wages the previous year in the agricultural/primary sector. The same methodology is then followed for the individuals who reported wage employment in the manufacturing/secondary sector and the service/tertiary sector.

Thereafter, I change the proxy of earnings from wages to household income and household consumption so as to avoid selective sampling bias. I use Equation 3 to analyse the impact of the English language on household earnings and household consumption for household heads in the agricultural/primary sector, for household heads in the manufacturing/secondary sector and finally, for household heads in the service/tertiary sector. The results are presented in Table 3.7 followed by an analysis.

Returns on individual's log hourly wages

The returns to fluent English skills on individuals' log hourly wages are statistically significant for all three sectors (Row a.i). This is expected since individuals who speak English in India are more likely to be in wage employment in all sectors. Within this category of wage employees, the returns to fluent English skills are lowest for individuals in the manufacturing/secondary sector and highest for individuals in the service/tertiary sector. While a fluent speaker in the manufacturing sector earns 10.2% more than a non-English speaker, a fluent speaker in the service sector earns 28.3% more. A fluent English-speaking wage employee in the primary sector earns 15.4% more than a non-English-speaking wage employee in the sector. I must reiterate that these returns to English skills reflected for the individuals in the

Table 3.7 Returns to English-speaking skills by sector (2011)

a) Returns on Individuals' Log Hourly Wages

		Primary/ Agricultural Sector (1)	*Agriculture (1.1)*	*Secondary/ Manufacturing Sector (2)*	*Tertiary/ Service Sector (3)*
i.	*Fluent English*	0.154***	0.060	0.102**	0.283***
		(0.0492)	(0.0467)	(0.0520)	(0.0257)
ii.	*Little English*	0.003	0.004	−0.002	0.070***
		(0.0177)	(0.0179)	(0.0271)	(0.0146)
iii.	District Fixed Effects	Yes	Yes	Yes	Yes
iv.	R-Squared	0.589	0.581	0.533	0.447
v.	Observations	7,635	6,921	5,012	21,548

b) Returns on Household Heads' Log Hourly Wages

		Primary/ Agricultural Sector	*Agriculture*	*Secondary/ Manufacturing Sector*	*Tertiary/ Service Sector*
i.	*Fluent English*	0.129	0.029	0.104	0.267***
		(0.0933)	(0.1194)	(0.0813)	(0.0390)
ii.	*Little English*	−0.044	−0.044	−0.017	0.052**
		(0.0307)	(0.0313)	(0.0396)	(0.0220)
iii.	District Fixed Effects	Yes	Yes	Yes	Yes
iv.	R-Squared	0.636	0.622	0.597	0.491
v.	Observations	3,145	2,744	2,240	9,747

c) Returns on Households' Per Capita Income Last Year

		Primary/ Agricultural Sector	*Agriculture*	*Secondary/ Manufacturing Sector*	*Tertiary/ Service Sector*
i.	*Fluent English*	0.154	0.011	0.083	0.250***
		(0.1557)	(0.2057)	(0.1154)	(0.0430)
ii.	*Little English*	−0.020	−0.012	−0.056	0.060**
		(0.0541)	(0.0564)	(0.0484)	(0.0289)
iii.	District Fixed Effects	Yes	Yes	Yes	Yes
iv.	R-Squared	0.448	0.404	0.587	0.528
v.	Observations	3,124	2,722	2,235	9,739

d) Returns on Households' Per Capita Expenditure Last Year

		Primary/ Agricultural Sector	*Agriculture*	*Secondary/ Manufacturing Sector*	*Tertiary/ Service Sector*
i.	*Fluent English*	0.298**	0.187	0.076	0.171***
		(0.1236)	(0.1624)	(0.0736)	(0.0304)
ii.	*Little English*	0.082**	0.062	0.044	0.079***
		(0.0398)	(0.0438)	(0.0379)	(0.0182)
iii.	District Fixed Effects	Yes	Yes	Yes	Yes
iv.	R-Squared	0.441	0.405	0.541	0.524
v.	Observations	3,148	2,746	2,240	9,767

Notes: The sample consists of individuals, both male and female, aged 18–65 who reported as being household heads in India Human Development Survey-Round 2 (2011). For controls, the omitted caste group is Higher Caste. The omitted religion dummy is Hindu. The omitted educational attainment group is zero years of schooling completed. The omitted dummy for SSLC exam performance is those who reported valid blank i.e. did not give the SSLC exam (there were a few values not pertaining to any sub-category that needed to be cleaned or dropped). Asterisk denotes significance level (= 10%, ** = 5% and *** = 1%). Robust Standard Errors are shown in parenthesis.*

primary sector are only applicable to those who work in wage employment, and not the farmers who work in farm and non-farm businesses. Indeed, when I limit the primary sector sample to those who reported as only working in agriculture, the returns to English skills are insignificant (Row a.i, Column 1.1).

The returns to little English skills are insignificant for wage employees in all sectors except services. In other words, it is only in the service sectors that wage employees get a positive and statistically significant return of 7% to little English skills (Row a.ii).

Returns on household head's log hourly wages

Upon limiting the sample of wage earners to household heads, the results show that the returns to fluent English skills in the service sector are again high and extremely significant, with a fluent speaker earning 26.7% more than a non-English speaker in the industry (Row b.i). Contrary to the results for *all* wage employees in the primary and secondary sectors, for *household heads* in these two sectors there exist insignificant returns to fluent English.

We had already discovered that the returns to English skills on the wages of individuals in agriculture within the primary sector are not significant because most of these respondents are in non-wage farm businesses. However, for the sample of household heads, the effect of fluent English skills on wages in the non-agricultural primary sector is also insignificant. A possible explanation for this is the age of the household head sample. It can be expected that in wage employment, the returns to fluent English are higher for the younger cohort as compared to the older cohort. In the sample of 401 *household heads* in wage employment in the non-agricultural primary sector, only 90 were in the 18–35 age cohort, while the remaining 311 were in the 36–65 age cohort. The sample was thus dominated by the older cohort. On the contrary, in the sample of *all individuals* in wage employment in the non-agricultural primary sector (714 observations), 335 individuals belonged to the younger cohort, while 252 and 127 belonged to the 36–50 and 51–65 age cohorts respectively. In other words, younger people formed almost half the sample size.

On analysing the returns to fluent English in the non-agricultural primary sector categorised by age cohort (Appendix 5), I find that there are indeed statistically significant returns to fluent English amongst the younger cohort of non-agricultural primary sector wage earners. However, the returns amongst the older cohorts are negative and highly insignificant. This analysis holds true for the sample of *all individuals* in the sector as well for the limited sample of *household heads*. While in the former sample the younger cohort constituted almost half the sample size, in the latter sample the majority of the household heads belonged to the older age group. Therefore, the insignificant returns to fluent English on wages for household heads in the non-agricultural primary sector, as well as in the overall primary sector, is fathomable.

Similarly, contrary to its effect on the wages of *all* individuals in the manufacturing sector, English language plays no statistically relevant role in determining the wages of *household heads*. However, the sample's industry category, rather than age cohort, explains the insignificance for this sector. For *all individuals* earning wages in the manufacturing sector, the significant returns to fluent English were in the beverage and tobacco manufacturing and leather manufacturing industries. The sample of *household heads* incorporated only one individual with fluent English skills in the beverage and tobacco manufacturing industry, and only three individuals with fluent skills in leather manufacturing. This extremely limited sample size paves the way for inconsistent results. It is therefore reasonable to prefer the specification provided in Row a.i, Column 3 (rather than Row b.i, Column 3), and construe that manufacturing sector wage employees do benefit from fluent English. However, these benefits are not as high as those for service sector wage earners.

The returns to little English skills on wages of household heads were again statistically insignificant for all sectors, barring services. A household head in the tertiary sector with little English skills earns 5.2% more than a household head in the same sector with no English skills (Row b.ii, Column 3).

Returns on household's per capita income last year

Moving on to the impact of English skills on household income, I find that fluent as well as little proficiency in the language have no significant effects in the primary/agricultural and secondary/manufacturing sectors. This was expected since the sample is no longer circumscribed to those in wage employment – an area of employment English speakers are predominantly attracted to.

As anticipated, a household where the head is employed in the service sector and can speak English fluently earns 25% higher per capita income than a household where the head is in the same sector but does not know English. The increase in the per capita income of a household in which the head has little English skills and works in the service sector is 6%.

Returns on household's per capita expenditure last year

On per capita expenditure, English language skills – both fluent and little – have statistically significant returns within the primary and service sectors. English, again, plays no statistical role in explaining the consumption of a household with a head involved in the manufacturing sector. Even within the primary sector, English is not a factor behind explaining the per capita expenditure in an agricultural household.

My results for the effect of English on earnings – wages, household income and household consumption – consistently reflect that the English language plays a significant role in explaining earnings in the service sector. Even in wage employment, where English significantly impacted all three sectors, the language's impact was noticeably higher within the service sector. In other words, service industries are the ones that are influenced the most by the English language. This finding is consistent with the theoretical conceptualisation that the contemporary dominant effect of the English language in India can be attributed to the country's reliance on the service sector.

We can thereby conclude that English plays a dominant role in positively influencing earnings at an individual level in India, particularly within the service sector. Since 53.7% of India's average economic growth in the 2000–2010 decade is attributed to services,[29] the English language inevitably plays a role in that growth.[30]

English language and state growth in India

> *I do not deny the importance of other languages. But, I stress the importance of English language as the international language of communication because knowledge is gained either by experience, learning and perception or through association and reasoning.*
>
> – (Chew Ging Lee, 2012)

Having established that the English language plays a significant role in determining earnings, especially in the service sector jobs, we now focus on whether the language has a positive relationship with the economic growth of Indian states. It is imperative for readers to note here that, unlike the earnings estimation – where we interpreted the number of the coefficient as well as the notation/sign on the coefficient on the independent variable English – in growth regression we must only interpret the notation. This is because growth estimations are extremely sensitive to the controls and proxies one uses in the estimation model, and the omitted relevant variable is always a concern. Limitations in data, in terms of quantity as well as quality, are another concern. Therefore, the sole purpose of this chapter is to establish whether the coefficient on English skills as an independent variable is positive or not.

The period of growth that this book concentrates on is 2005 to 2014. The reasons for choosing this specific period are threefold: first, it provides the most contemporary reflection of Indian state growth; second, since the earliest English skills data is for the year 2005, it would be reasonable to take 2005 as the base year; third, the most reliable state-level growth data – available from the Ministry of Statistics and Programme Implementation

(MOSPI), Government of India – unfortunately has significant variations in its series of state-level growth records over the years, which makes compilation difficult. Growth data at constant prices cannot not be used since the base year changes in each data sheet. Surprisingly, data at current prices also shows variation on different MOSPI series. For instance, the per capita growth in the net state domestic product (NSDP) at current prices of Andhra Pradesh for 2006–2007 is recorded as 8.72% in the 2004–2005 MOSPI series. The same is puzzlingly recorded as 11.44% in the MOSPI 1999–2000 series. Given these large variations, it would not be suitable to compile these different series of datasets and only use one. Since data for English is available for the years 2005 and 2011, I use the 2004–2005 MOSPI series that reports the state domestic products for the Indian states from 2004 until 2014 at the constant 2004–2005 prices.

Out of the 36 states/union territories in India, this study covers only 31, since data on English skills is not available for Lakshadweep and Andaman and Nicobar Island, and data on the growth of the gross state domestic product (GSDP) is not available for Daman and Diu or Dadra and Nagar Haveli. Furthermore, Telangana was not a separate state during a majority of the time-period considered, and therefore, all relevant data for Telangana is incorporated in that for Andhra Pradesh.

There are only a few pieces of literature analysing the growth of Indian states using a cross-sectional lens. My primary estimation method is adapted from a growth study by Montek Singh Ahluwalia published in 2002, titled "State-Level Performance Under Economic Reforms in India,"[31] since this paper is one of the few focusing on a cross-sectional Indian state-growth analysis. Moreover, similar to my study, it focuses on a ten-year time-period of the Indian states' growth. The fact that he was a member of the Planning Commission of the Government of India at the time of writing the paper gives it further authentic clout over similar studies. In this study, Ahluwalia documented the performance of 14 major states of India in the post-reform period 1991–1992 to 1998–1999 and compared it to the performance in the previous decade. In doing so, he empirically investigated and listed the determinants of growth in the states of India post-1991 reforms. Both his estimation equation as well as the resultant list of determinants are of interest to this chapter of the book.

Using the average of the growth in the GSDP as his dependent variable, Ahluwalia ran *separate* regressions for each independent variable that could theoretically explain Indian states' growth rate. These variables included Investment Ratios (compiled by the Centre for Monitoring the Indian Economy in their capex database) for the year 1995,[32] Plan Expenditure,[33] Human Resources (proxied by Literacy Rate) and Quality of Infrastructure. His equation model was thus the following:

$$Growth_{1991-1999} = \alpha + \beta_1 X_{1991} \tag{4}$$

where, $Growth_{1991-1999}$ was the average of the growth in the GSDP of the 14 states from 1991 to 1999, α was the constant from the regression and X was the independent variable of interest. Data for all variables X pertained to the base year 1991, barring an investment ratio for which data pertained to the year 1995–1996.

Upon estimating the previous equation for all the aforementioned variables, Ahluwalia found that only investment ratio and three indices of infrastructure – namely, percentage of villages electrified in the base year, per capita energy consumption and telecommunication density – played a role in determining the growth of Indian states from 1991 to 1999. Furthermore, he found that human capital did not show significant effects until it was multiplied with the capex investment ratio into a composite variable. In other words, his data reflected that the response of state growth to higher investment rate was greater the larger the literacy variable, thus building in a positive interaction effect.

Adapting and modifying Ahluwalia's method of estimation (Equation 4), I approximate the following equation to conduct a preliminary analysis of the relationship of the English language with the state growth in India:

$$Growth_{2005-2014} = \alpha + \beta_1 English_{2005} \qquad (5)$$

where, $GSDP_{2004-2014}$ is the average of the growth in the GSDP of 31 Indian states from 2005 till 2014 and $English_{2005}$ is the proportion of English speakers in each state (proxy for English skills) in the base year 2005.

Data on the average of the year on year growth in GSDP is accessed from the Ministry of Statistics and Programme Implementation (MOSPI), Government of India. A comment on the problems with the state-level SDP data is appropriate at this stage. Ideally the GSDP data for individual states should be completely consistent with the national account estimates for the GDP of India, so that the disaggregated picture of the economic performance at the state level is coherent with that of the country as a whole (as reported in the national accounts). Unfortunately, this consistency does not exist in the Indian context because, as Ahluwalia rightly explains, GSDP data is prepared by the statistics department of the government of each state, who vary in their methodologies for estimating, while national GDP data is presented in the national accounts.[34] Though problems related to the GSDP series are important, it should not stop us from using it to get an illustrative picture, if not representative. After all, as Ahluwalia points out, some Indian states are larger than most developing countries whose national accounts data have similar problems.[35] Such problems have not deterred researchers from doing cross-country growth analysis, and therefore following academic traditions I proceed with the analysis with a prior acknowledgement of the limitations.

Data on English skills of states is aggregated from the IHDS Round 1 dataset. Based on the conceptualisation presented at the initiation of this section of the book, it can be reasonably expected that the rate of absorption of knowledge of an economy – that aids economic growth – will be greater if the size of who has better command over English is larger. A good proxy of English skills would therefore be one that captures two dimensions: the fraction of the population that knows English and the level of English proficiency of these individuals. Fortunately, IHDS captures both dimensions. It not only gives us the fraction of the population that can speak in English, but it also categorises this population as fluent or little English speakers. The limitation, however, is that the quality of the level of English skills is debatable since it is based on the individuals' own perceptions of their English skills, rather than on a tested methodology (like an English exam score).

Despite the limitations with the state-level data, I use Equation 5 to run two regressions analysing the relationship between English language and GSDP growth in India. The dependent variable in each case is *Growth*, i.e. the average growth in GSDP from 2004 to 2014. The independent variables are *TEnglish* (proportion of English speakers, with fluent or little skills, in the states in 2005) and *FEnglish* (proportion of fluent English speakers in the states in 2005). The results are as follows (with asterisks representing significance: *** = significant at 1% level, ** = significant at 5% level and * = significant at 10%level, and p-values reported in parentheses):

I. $Growth = 8.021 + 0.0079\ TEnglish$ R^2=0.01
(0.63)

II. $Growth = 7.955 + 0.0361\ FEnglish$ R^2= 0.04
(0.26)

Though both variables for English skills in the regression have the expected positive signs, there appears to be no significant relationship between variation in growth across states and variation in total English-speaking skills across states. Although the coefficient on fluent English (*FEnglish*) is very much high (and economically large), it is still statistically insignificant. This could be due to the scarcity of the observations (limited to 31 states) or measurement error which makes the estimate imprecise.

Upon finding insignificant effects of human capital on growth in his paper analysing state-level growth in India, Ahluwalia argued that the role of human skills in India is not independent of the investment level, and that the two must interact with each other to generate positive responses pertaining to growth. A similar rationale can be used to explain the insignificance of English alone on the growth of states. As mentioned in the theoretical conceptualisation presented in the first part of this chapter, English affects growth through education by increasing the stock of knowledge. In other words, it is a form of human capital. Taking this into consideration, one can use Ahluwalia's argument that human capital skills in India – proxied by English language skills in this case – might not be independent of the investment level, and that the two must interact with each other to create a positive effect. To test this theory, I find data on state-level investment as a share of GSDP for the base year 2005 and analyse it with the data on English skills.

A note on the difficulty of finding state-level investment data is imperative here. State-level growth studies in India have suffered greatly due to the lack of investment data, since rate of investment is traditionally regarded as one of the most important determinants of growth in any economy. Investment is generally measured by the gross capital formation (GCF), which comprises gross fixed capital formation (GFCF) and change in stocks or inventories. At the national level, GFCF is used as the measurement of investment due to the fluctuating nature of inventories. At the state level, however, this information of GFCF is not that easily available. Though various reports, including those by the National Statistical Commission (2001) and High Level Committee (Government of India, 2009), have analysed and recommended several measures for improvements in the estimation of state-level private and public GFCF in India, the data accessibility is still an issue. This is due to the non-availability of details on state-level capital expenditure in private corporation and household sectors.

Ahluwalia, who used that capex database, stated that this database was the only one that has information regarding investment expenditures since 1995. The dataset, however, has various limitations that Ahluwalia highlighted in his study. First, the data excludes investment in the household and unorganised sectors, which constitutes 33% of the total investment in the India economy. Second, the investment expenditure reported is the total expenditure for completing each project, and not the expenditure by each project in a year. Due to this, the data available in capex captures investment made in previous years in all ongoing projects as well as the expected investment in the future years on these projects. Third, the data is collected from multiple sources such as press releases and newspaper accounts, thereby making the basis of investment values on non-comparable prices. Apart from these important limitations, the subscription cost to the dataset is steep, thereby making it inaccessible. While Ahluwalia, who was a member of the Planning Commission of India while writing the paper, got access to the dataset, researchers like myself can only get access through subscription. Given the database's glaring limitations, thc high cost of access seemed unreasonable to pay.

Fortunately, the Government of India, in their 2009 report, estimated the state-level private investment at current prices for the year 2004–2005, thereby enabling an estimation of the state-level gross fixed capital formation (GFCF). This publication is of great use to this research, since the base year of my study coincides with the year of the investment data availability.

Moreover, since my measure of the growth in GSDP is at the constant 2004–2005 prices, it is comparable to the investment data that is also measured at the 2004–2005 prices, thereby eliminating the bias caused by inflation.

I estimate regression equations using growth of GSDP as the dependent variable and a composite variable obtained by multiplying average English speakers with the total gross fixed capital formation as a share of total GSDP in the base year (coded *GFCF*). This multiplicative form indicates that the higher the English skills of a state, the greater the response of growth to investment. The results of the regression are as follows:

III. $Growth = 7.650 + 0.0005^{*}\,(GFCF \times TEnglish)$ $\qquad R^2 = 0.11$
$\qquad\qquad\qquad\qquad (0.08)$

IV. $Growth = 7.762 + 0.0014^{**}\,(GFCF \times FEnglish)$ $\qquad R^2 = 0.13$
$\qquad\qquad\qquad\qquad (0.04)$

The inclusion of a composite variable that permits an interactive effect of English skills and gross fixed capital formation as a share of the GSDP of the states improves the explanatory power of each of the English variables. While total English-speaking skills' interaction with investment is at a 10% significance level, fluent English-speaking skills' interaction is at a 5% significance level. Both variables for English have the expected positive signs. In other words, the empirical results highlight that in India, the response of growth to investment in a state is greater the higher the proportion of English speakers. The degree of this response is further increased in states where the proportion of fluent English speakers is higher. Therefore, the English language is positively related to the growth of the state domestic product in India, with the growth of a state that encompasses a larger proportion of English speakers reacting more to investment, than that of a state with fewer English speakers.

State-level growth by sectors

As mentioned previously, India's growth has been driven by the service sector. The Planning Commission Data reports that the aggregate of the average growth of GSDP between 2005–2006 and 2013–2014 was again the highest in the service sector of the country (as evidenced in Table 3.8). The average growth rate of the total GSDP in services was 9.07%, while it was 7.45% and 3.97% in manufacturing and agriculture respectively.

I had previously suggested that the theoretical underpinning of the relationship between the English language and economic growth is more likely to fit the Indian context (relative to less service dependent developing countries like China) due to the country's reliance on the service sector for growth. For the conceptualisation to stand true, I now empirically substantiate that the

Table 3.8 Growth rate (%) of GSDP of sectors at constant 2004–2005 prices: 2005–2006 to 2013–2014

State	*Service Sector*	*Manufacturing Sector*	*Agriculture and Allied Sector*
Andaman and Nicobar Island	12.96	2.38	3.48
Andhra Pradesh	9.75	8.73	5.07
Arunachal Pradesh	8.91	6.78	3.77
Assam	8.21	2.1	3.65
Bihar	11.17	6.65	4.31
Chandigarh	7.9	4.89	-3.87
Chhattisgarh	9.39	3.39	6.8
Delhi	11.39	4.77	3.93
Goa	15.42	5.73	0.15
Gujarat	11.45	9.57	5.36
Haryana	11.68	6.22	3.67
Himachal Pradesh	10	12.68	4.47
Jammu and Kashmir	8.9	7.36	1.93
Jharkhand	2.02	8.98	8.59
Karnataka	9.18	5.93	3.73
Kerala	9.63	6.84	-0.52
Madhya Pradesh	8.73	7.8	9.56
Maharashtra	9.83	7.93	5.16
Manipur	9.46	7.07	2.45
Meghalaya	9.17	21.97	2.85
Mizoram	9.81	10.89	6.34
Nagaland	9.58	9.84	4.02
Odisha	9.25	11.62	2.75
Puducherry	14.32	7.93	9.04
Punjab	8.81	9.78	1.49
Rajasthan	9.39	6.78	5.27
Sikkim	8.29	149.23	7.27
Tamil Nadu	10.48	9.08	4.42
Tripura	9.66	11.8	8.1
Uttar Pradesh	8.9	5.54	3.26
Uttarakhand	12.68	22.07	2.84
West Bengal	8.87	5.6	2.53
India Total	**9.07**	**7.45**	**3.97**

Source: Planning Commission of India Data, Government of India.

English language has a positive and statistically significant relationship with the growth rate of GSDP of services across the Indian states from 2005 to 2014.

In order to do so, I ran six regressions – the first three show the relationship between total English in a state (*TEnglish*) and the growth rate of GSDP segregated by sectors, while the latter three show the relationship between fluent English speakers in a state (*FEnglish*) and the growth rate of GSDP across sectors. The results are presented in Table 3.9.

Table 3.9 Relationship between English language and the growth rate of GSDP segregated by sectors

Total English Speakers			
	Co-efficient	*p-value*	*R-Squares*
Growth of GSDP of Agriculture and Allied Sector	-0.0464**	0.03	0.16
Growth of GSDP of Manufacturing Sector	0.1538	0.43	0.02
Growth of GSDP of Service Sector	0.0213	0.20	0.13
Fluent English Speakers			
	Co-efficient	*p-value*	*R-Squares*
Growth of GSDP of Agricultural and Allied Sector	-0.0087	0.84	0.00
Growth of GSDP of Manufacturing Sector	0.2815	0.46	0.02
Growth of GSDP of Service Sector	0.0674**	0.03	0.15

Source: Tabulated by using a collated dataset with data points from Planning Commission of India data and IHDS Round 2.

As anticipated, the English language and the growth rate of GSDP of services have a positive relationship. While the coefficient on *TEnglish* is statistically not significant, the coefficient on *FEnglish* is at 5% significance level. It is therefore safe to construe that there exists a positive and statistically significant relationship between the proportion of fluent English speakers in a state and the growth rate of the GSDP of services.

Interestingly, the notations on both the variables of English for agriculture and allied sector state-level growth were negative. While the relationship between fluent English and state-level agriculture sector growth was statistically insignificant, that of total English was statistically significant at 5% significance level. The implication of this finding is that if the total proportion of English speakers is higher in a state, the agricultural sector growth of the state will be less. An explanation for this negative relationship between the language and growth in the agricultural sector is that the human capital of English enables individuals to move out of agricultural jobs into more sought-after professions, specifically in services.

Contrary to the results for growth in state-level services and agriculture sectors, the data does not reflect a significant relationship between growth in GSDP of the manufacturing sector and the English language (both total and fluent). Though the notations on both the variables of English were positive for the growth in manufacturing sector GSDP, they were statistically insignificant. One can argue that the effects of physical capital rather than human capital are higher for the manufacturing sector's growth, and the latter must interact with the former to generate positive responses. Using a composite variable obtained by multiplying the proportion of English speakers per state, both total and fluent, with the GFCF as a share of GSDP for the year 2004–2005, I ran two regressions which yielded the following results:

V. *Manufacturing Growth* = 3.237 + 0.0070** (GFCF × *TEnglish*) $R^2 = 0.17$
(0.02)

VI. *Manufacturing Growth* = 6.178 + 0.0178** (*GFCF* × *FEnglish*) $R^2 = 0.15$
(0.03)

Indeed, the composite variable obtained by multiplying the proportion of English speakers (both fluent and total) with total GFCF as a share of GSDP has a positive and statistically significant relationship with the manufacturing sector growth of the states. In other words, in an Indian state, the response of growth in the manufacturing sector to physical capital investment is greater if the proportion of English speakers is higher.

From these results we can conclude that English language does play a role in the economic growth of India from a cross-state analysis. While fluent English skills have a direct and positive relationship with the growth in services, fluent and total English skills share an indirect relationship with manufacturing sector growth (by increasing the impact of investment). Since the Indian economy's growth is dictated by services, followed by manufacturing, it is reasonable to construe that English has a positive relationship with the growth of India.[36]

Summary of the economic effects of the English language

There are large and statistically significant returns to English language speaking skills in India. Hourly wages are on an average 34% higher for individuals who speak fluent English and 7% higher for individuals who speak little English relative to those who speak no English. This finding is further substantiated by the effect of English on household income, where a household with a fluent English-speaking head earns approximately 33% more and a household with a little English-speaking head earns approximately 7% more than a household with a non-English-speaking head. The expenditures of households with English-speaking heads are also significantly higher than those with a non-English-speaking head (though the effects of fluent language ability on consumption are lower than that on income, probably due to saving habits of households). The returns to

English are the most significant in service sector jobs – the sector that is predominantly responsible for the economic growth of India.

The state-level growth in India also shares a positive relationship with this language. Particularly, the response of the growth in GSDP to physical capital investment is higher the larger the proportion of English speakers in the states. Furthermore, English directly affects the service sector growth of states and indirectly – via physical capital – affects the manufacturing sector growth. Given that India benefited most from service sector growth, it is reasonable to conclude that English indeed plays a positive role in the economic growth of India.

This chapter of the book is the second to use a nationally representative sample to estimate the economic returns to English language skills on wages in India, and the first to deduce the economic relationship of the language with sectors and state growth. No study prior to this has attempted to quantify the impact of the English language on state and sector growth of India. Though reverse causality is a limitation that readers need to note, even without the causal interpretation, my results highlight a positive association between the English language and economic indicators, including wages and growth. This suggests that individuals and policy-makers should consider language skills as an important factor when making human capital decisions for the betterment of their wages and the country's growth.

Notes

1 Yes, it has been a long, six years journey from the seed idea to a doctorate to a book.
2 Lee, C. G. (2012). English language and economic growth: Cross-country empirical evidence. *Journal of Economic and Social Studies*, 2(1), 5–20.
3 To justify this statement, Lee cited Aghion and Howitt, 1992; Grossmann and Helpman, 1991; Jones, 1995; Romer, 1990.
4 Lee, English language and economic growth: Cross-country empirical evidence.
5 Keller, W. (2002). Geographic localization of international technology diffusion. *American Economic Review*, 92, 120–142.
6 Lee, English language and economic growth: Cross-country empirical evidence.
7 Ibid.
8 *The Telegraph*. (2017, February 9). *Mapped: Where to go if you can't be bothered to learn the language*. Retrieved September 2, 2018, from www.telegraph.co.uk/travel/maps-and-graphics/mapped-english-speaking-countries/
9 Lin, Long live China's boom.
10 Education First. (2018). *EF English proficiency index*. Retrieved November 2, 2018, from www.ef.com/__/~/media/centralefcom/epi/downloads/full-reports/v8/ef-epi-2018-english.pdf
11 Ibid.
12 Lee, English language and economic growth: Cross-country empirical evidence.
13 While Lee used TOEFL total score mean of examinees as the proxy for English language proficiency, Arcand and Grin approximated it as a stock of English knowledge by multiplying the average TOEFL score with the number of people who sat for it in each country.

14 Grin, F. (2001). English as economic value: Facts and fallacies. *World Englishes*, *20*(1), 65–78.
15 Azam, Chin, and Prakash, op.cit.
16 Kapur, S., and Chakraborty, T. (2008). *English language premium: Evidence from a policy experiment in India*. Unpublished manuscript. St. Louis: Department of Economics, Washington University.
17 Ford, S., and Strange, R. (1999). Where do Japanese manufacturing firms invest within Europe, and why? *Transnational Corporations*, *8*(1), 117–140.
18 Coleman, H. (2011). The English language in development. *MEXTESOL Journal*, *35*(1).
19 Suárez, S. L. (2005). Does English rule? Language instruction and economic strategies in Singapore, Ireland and Puerto Rico. *Comparative Politics*, *37*(4), 459–478.
20 *The Economic Times*. (2016, April 8). *India's rank unchanged at 19th among top 30 exporters*. Retrieved October 29, 2018, from https://economictimes.indiatimes.com/news/economy/foreign-trade/indias-rank-unchanged-at-19th-among-top-30-exporters/articleshow/51745091.cms
21 Quote retrieved from Daily O. (2018, March 21). *13 ways of looking at English: This language gets work done in India*. Retrieved October 29, 2018, from www.dailyo.in/arts/english-language-day-india-obsession-works/story/1/22990.html
22 Azam, Chin, and Prakash, op.cit.
23 The square of age is taken since the relationship of earnings with age is exponential. This is because after a certain age, an individual's income begins to diminish due to factors like less productivity and retirement.
24 I have taken the *log* of earnings as the independent variable so as to estimate the *percentage* change, rather than unit change, in earnings.
25 Though it falls outside the scope of this book, it is interesting to see that the regression yielded a positive notation on the square of age, while in common wisdom it is assumed that the relationship between earnings and age is exponential. A probable reason for this positive notation is the selection bias caused by limiting the sample to the working age population of 18 to 65. Furthermore, the regression yielded a dramatic convex relationship between the level of education and earnings, while the common belief is that in developing countries, labour-market returns to education are highest for the primary level and lower thereafter, thereby paving the way for a concave relationship. This finding is in line with the findings of Colclough, Kingdon and Patrinos's (2010) study *The Changing Pattern of Wage Returns to Education and its Implications*, which concluded that in recent times (1990s and early 2000s) the relationship between earnings and level of education has indeed become a convex one.
26 Though NCAER and the University of Maryland re-interviewed 83% of the households (plus any split households) interviewed in IHDS Round 1, the sample is slightly different due to the loss of 6,911 households and the addition of 2,134 new households.
27 In previous estimations, while a few dummies were insignificant, the independent variables as a whole were significant. In the estimation of earnings for women, however, religion and failed/repeated year are insignificant.
28 Philip Powell-Davies for the British Council. (2015). *The social and economic case for developing English skills*. Retrieved October 29, 2018, from www.britishcouncil.org.eg/en/symposium/thought-pieces/social-and-economic-case-developing-english-skills
29 Mukherjee, *The service sector in India*.

30 The limitations pertaining to the empirical substantiation of the language-earning relationship presented in this book are provided in Appendix 6.
31 Ahluwalia, M. S. (2002). State-level performance under economic reforms in India. In A. O. Krueger (Ed.), *Economic policy reforms and the Indian economy* (pp. 91–122). Chicago: University of Chicago Press.
32 Investment data pertains to the year 1995–1996 (and not the base year 1991–1992) because prior to that CMIE did not gather investment-related data.
33 Plan Expenditure, in the Indian context, refers to expenditures on new projects commenced in a particular five-year period, and includes both capital expenditures and current expenditures.
34 Ahluwalia, *State-level performance under economic reforms in India.*
35 Ibid.
36 The limitations pertaining to the empirical substantiation of the language-growth relationship presented in this book are provided in Appendix 7.

4
THE ENGLISH LANGUAGE AND INCLUSIVE GROWTH

Language-inclusivity link: cultural capital conduit

It is we the English-knowing Indians that have enslaved India. The curse of the nation will not rest upon the English but upon us.

– (Mahatma Gandhi, 1909)[1]

Every coin has two sides. English might be a boon for economic growth, yet its negative effects cannot be ignored. On one hand, we have peripherists like Viniti Vaish who view English as a mode of decolonisation that empowers those that were historically and linguistically subalternised.[2] They believe that English provides the previously linguistically disenfranchised people access to the linguistic capital that has become essential within the market forces of globalisation, and ergo they view English as a medium of opportunity. On the other hand, we have sociolinguists including Badri Raina who emphasise the role of the English language in socially quelling non-English speakers in Indian society, thereby promoting the view that English is a medium of repression. Evidently, the social impact of English in India has been a debatable issue. It is therefore surprising that this debate has not expanded its ambit to include the economic and monetary subordination of non-English speakers, given that such economic subservience can perpetuate into non-inclusivity of the benefits of economic growth.

As with the validation of any theory, the initiation must be with a conceptual underpinning. How does the English language, theoretically, correlate to inclusive growth?

A theoretical underpinning provided in past literature for the language-inclusive growth relationship is Pierre Bourdieu's concept of cultural capital. Bourdieu introduced this concept in 1974, whereby he expanded the category of capital to something more than just the economic and identified culture as a form of capital. Cultural capital was defined as consisting of familiarity with the dominant culture in a society. In 1977, he included language as a prominent component of cultural capital, specifically the ability to understand and use the "educated" language.[3]

As with all the other capitals, Bourdieu's concern in relation to cultural capital was with its continual transmission and accumulation in ways that perpetuate social inequalities. In the case of language, the mode through which the inequality perpetuated was the education sector. His concept of cultural capital moved away from the common notion that attributed academic success or failure to natural aptitudes, such as intelligence and giftedness. Instead, the concept associated school success with the amount and type of cultural capital inherited from the family milieu, including the ability to use the "educated" language.

He propagated that socio-economic class determines the degree of cultural capital one possesses, particularly the ability to converse in the "educated" language. Someone from a low socio-economic background could lack the proficiency in the "educated" language. Yet the education systems of the society are likely to assume equitable possession of this cultural capital of language, thereby resulting in inefficiency in "pedagogic transmission" or teaching. Consequently, the lower-class students are disadvantaged due to difficulties in understanding, which eventually gets reflected in their credentials.

The credentials are, however, assumed to be meritocratic and legitimate by the academic institutions as well as job markets, hence paving the way for the legitimisation of class distinction. In other words, those that do not possess the cultural capital of the "educated" language due to relatively poor socio-economic backgrounds are disadvantaged in academic institutions. This gets reflected in their credentials and is misinterpreted as their lack of ability and talent. This axiomatically paves the way for disadvantages on the job market, further embedding the social/economic class disparity, hence hindering inclusive growth. The children of these non-English speakers who fare badly in school and the labour market in turn are disadvantaged in school since they fail to receive the cultural capital of language. And thus, the vicious cycle goes on, resulting in the prevalence of inter-generational occupational tiers.

If one adds Michel Foucault's knowledge-power nexus to this dynamic – in which the scholar propagates an inextricable relation between knowledge and power, as "knowledge is always an exercise of power and power always a function of knowledge"[4] – the situation of those who don't know the educated language becomes direr. A lack of the educated language would perpetuate into a lack of knowledge and power, which would limit what non-English speakers do, and how they think and act.

Now, though Bourdieu's concept of cultural capital is a rational theory to explain the negative relationship between the English language (which is undoubtedly the "educated" language in India) and inclusive growth, as well as for the persistence of inter-generational occupational tiers, its premise might fail to empirically apply to the case of India. In India, even non-English speakers perform well in school. This is substantiated by the fact that in the CBSE 10th grade national examination results of 2014, while only 63 out of the 306 students who gave the examinations from the private, English-speaking Delhi Public School (North branch) scored the perfect score of 10 CGPA, 45 out of 185 students who sat for the examinations from the state-owned, predominantly non-English-speaking Kendriya Vidyalaya School (DRDO branch) got the perfect score.[5] The surprising and noteworthy part is that some, if not all, of the CBSE exam subjects are in English, yet most students of Kendriya Vidyalaya find it difficult to communicate in the language.

The fascinating question that arises is how are non-English speakers writing exams in English, and faring well in them on top of that? Evidently, India's education system is a special case that has contradicted Bourdieu's premise, yet it has substantiated his conclusion. Perhaps it is in the analysis of this irony of non-English speakers having the ability to write exams conducted in English that the solution to the lack of inclusivity lies. This irony will be further addressed in the next section of this book.

Though the premise of cultural capital theory does not completely apply to India, it is nevertheless an important theory as it underlines the notion that the inequality of income is caused by the inequality of language skills and can persist over generations. This is indeed the case in India. It further brings to light the irony that exists in India, the analysis of which is essential for the resolution of the paradoxical relationship between the English language and growth (economic and inclusive).

Language-inclusivity link: ratio theory

English is useful but our obsessions with everything English is perhaps not.

– (Anil Swarup, 2018)[6]

Since the premise of cultural capital theory fails to completely apply to India, the concept does not provide the required theoretical explanation for the negative effect of the English language on inclusive growth, specifically in India.[7] One must derive the said conceptualisation to explain the negative correlation between the English language and inclusive growth that can be applicable to the special case of India.

In Chapter 3, we recognised that the rationale for the English language's positive effect on service-driven growth of countries is due to its role as the medium for absorption of new knowledge in today's globalised world. What now needs to be focused on is the spread and reach of this medium of absorption, i.e. the ratio of English speakers to non-English speakers.

Chew Ging Lee, one of the few authors to have considered the role of the English language directly on economic growth, conceded that though the mean score of TOELF examinees as a proxy of English captured the level of English proficiency, it did not fully capture the fraction of the population who can speak English. His study underlines that economic growth depends on the quality of English skills, whereby countries with a higher level of English proficiency among a fraction of its population are likely to grow faster. His recommendation for growth was that not all workers in a country need to master English –

> what I would like to stress is that in a country a fraction of workers must be fluent in English. This group of workers will gain access to the new knowledge and then they can translate the learned knowledge into the local language to allow the learned knowledge to reach a wider audience.[8]

However, what if, instead of using English to learn and then translate this new knowledge into the local languages to increase access, the English speakers use the language to bar access? Furthermore, what if the proportion of these English-speakers with the ability to block knowledge access is very small compared to the proportion of non-English speakers? The answer is non-inclusive growth.

Once newly created knowledge is absorbed by the English-speaking fraction of the population of developing countries, including India, the stock of knowledge increases, resulting in an increase in human capital and economic growth. However, if the knowledge is not shared with the non-English-speaking population, the English speakers not only gain an elite status, but they also become the sole beneficiaries of the prosperity that the economic growth brings with it. The situation is worsened when the English-speakers form a very small fraction of the population (i.e. when the ratio of English speakers to non-English speakers is low), as the consequence is the exclusion of a large proportion of the population from growth (see Figure 4.1).

This *Ratio Theory* is applicable to the case of India. Since India is a developing country with a 28.7% English-speaking population, its human capital stock increase is largely through absorption of knowledge founded in developed countries. Since the fraction of English-speakers is small, 72.3% of the population has to rely on the dissemination of new knowledge through translation. This translation, however, is not taking place, and the non-English speakers are instead getting barred from access and the resulting benefits, resulting in non-inclusive growth. Once the linguistic inequality perpetuates into monetary inequality, the vicious inter-generational cycle gains momentum.

The fact that India's growth was largely driven by the service sector (as addressed in the previous section of this book) helps validate this framework. The positive economic growth stems from the commodity (in this

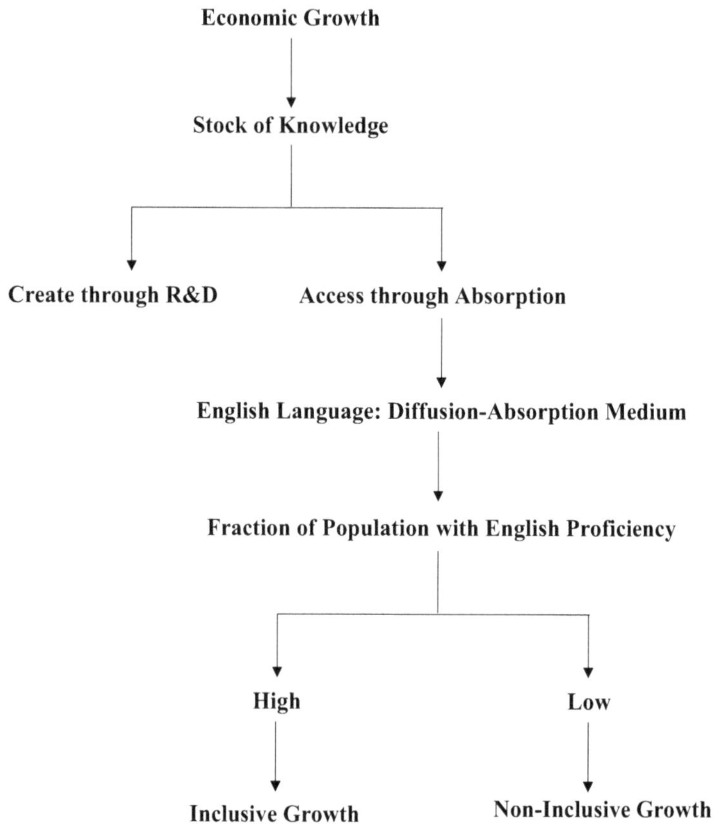

Figure 4.1 Relationship between English language and inclusive growth
Source: Compiled by author.

case service) demand in the service sector; however, the negative inclusive growth stems from the labour demand in the service sector. Since labour demand is derived demand, the workers demanded are ones who fit the service sector requirements. Kochar et al. highlighted that there exists a strong focus on skill-intensive services and higher education in the service sector of India, while the majority of the population remains unskilled and poorly educated.[9] English language is one such skill since it is an explicit stock of knowledge in the service sector. Workers with English-speaking skills are consequently the demanded ones. The elitism associated with English due to the historical heritage further makes these workers more attractive to the local employers. Therefore, English speakers add and benefit from the service-driven growth, while non-English speakers are excluded.

Unfortunately, very little empirical work has been done to prove this negative correlation between the English language and inclusive growth, and none of these works have focused on India. These works have concentrated on the broader concepts of development and inequalities, rather than the specific concept of inclusive growth. Nonetheless, since inclusive growth is a subset of development, the findings of these studies are relevant.

Hywel Coleman's 2011 paper titled "The English Language in Development" is one such study that sheds lights on the negative impact of English on development. The paper begins with a brief discussion of how understanding of the concept of "development" has changed over the last six decades and concurs with Amartya Sen's view of development as freedom. The paper then examines different roles that have been given to English: for employability, in international mobility and as a key for unlocking development opportunities. The paper concludes that while there is evidence that English is important for these roles, some caution is needed, as English can be dangerously overused and its role can be exaggerated – as in the case of India – hindering individual and national development.[10]

Lamb and Coleman in "Literacy in English and the Transformation of Self and Society in Post-Soeharto Indonesia," using Indonesia as the case study, highlighted the negative impact of the spread of English on development. The work states that in Indonesia, propagated by government, demanded by employers, broadcasted by the media, imposed by schools and encouraged by parents (similar to the scenario in India), English occupies an important space in the mind-set of many, going far beyond its actual practical value in daily life. Drawing on two empirical studies in Sumatra, one a large-scale evaluation of educational provision, the other a case study of English learning at school, the paper shows how the degree of investment that young Indonesians make in the language is not solely a matter of personal agency but is constrained by inequalities in the distribution of social and economic capital. The research concludes that "unless radical curriculum changes are introduced, the spread of English may in the long-term only serve to deepen these inequalities."[11]

It is interesting to note that most of the literature addressing the negative impact of the English language on development – in the economic rather than the socio-psychological sense – is quite recent. This increasing interest substantiates the growing role of the English language in the dynamics of today's economy. It is thus surprising that scholars have not yet attempted to investigate the negative economic impacts caused by English in India (though socio-psychological and linguistic impacts have been studied), given that the country attaches excessive value to the language due to its heritage.

Income strata of non-English speakers

Accepting that English is the national language would have benefits that far outweigh soothing the emotions of Indian

> *nationalism. It is to emphasize this point that Chandra Bhan Prasad has built a temple to the Goddess English in an impoverished village in the northern state of Uttar Pradesh. People like Mr. Prasad . . . want to liberate the poorest segment of the population, the Dalits, through the extraordinary power of English.*
>
> – (Manu Joseph, 2011)[12]

It has been established that there are substantial returns to the English language in India. Another interpretation of this result is that the hourly wage of an individual with no English-speaking ability is on an average 34% less than that of an individual with fluent English-speaking ability, and 7% less than that of an individual with little English-speaking ability. While this finding partially substantiates the disadvantage faced by the non-English speakers in the Indian economy, it does not do justice in explaining the degree of that handicap. After all, an individual could earn 34% less than someone and still have a comfortable standard of living.

In order to shed light on the degree of disadvantage faced by non-English speakers in India, let us focus on a nationally representative analysis built on IHDS Round 2 data. Particularly, let us look at the income strata that the non-English speakers predominantly belong to and the probability of their progress to a higher stratum.

The National Council of Applied Economic Research-Centre for Macro Consumer Research (NCAER-CMCR) conducted an income analysis using their door-to-door National Survey of Household Income and Expenditure, which covered 97,755 households in India. Using the survey data, NCAER-CMCR stratified the entire country, approximating 240 million households, according to income. The stratification yielded four categories of households based on their annual income – the *deprived* who earned below INR 1.5 lakh (approximately £1500); the *aspirers* who earned between INR 1.5 lakh to 3.4 lakh (approximately £1500-£3400); the *middle class* who earned between INR 3.4 lakh to 17 lakh (approximately £3400-£17000); and the *rich* who earned above INR 17 lakh. The diagrammatical representation of the classification is reproduced in Figure 4.2.

To deduce the stratum that non-English speakers predominantly fall into, segregation of the IHDS Round 2 sample into the aforementioned income strata is required. The disaggregation of the working age population, as per their response to questions regarding household income, yields that, unsurprisingly, a majority of the sample belongs to a deprived household.

The NCAER-CMCR tabulation highlighted that 56% of individuals belonged to a deprived household in 2010. The IHDS Round 2 data for 2011 reflects an inflated figure of approximately 74% (see Figure 4.3). Since the NCAER-CMCR analysis has a larger sample size, it is reasonable to

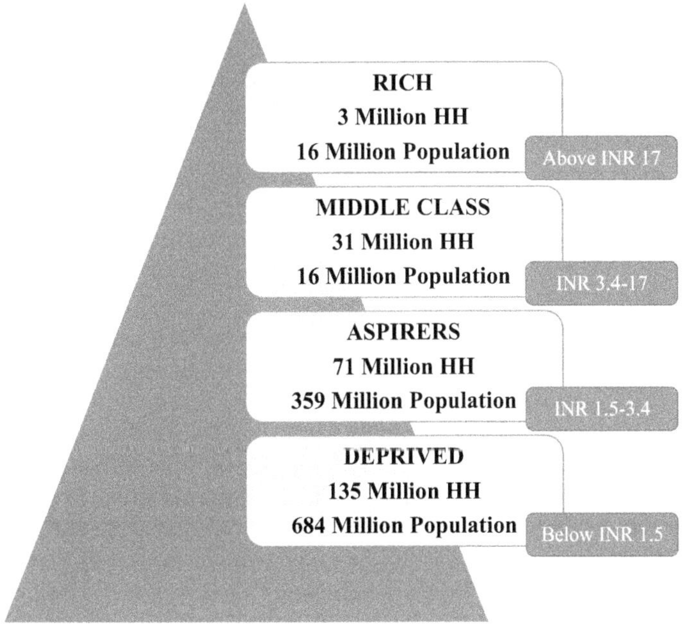

Figure 4.2 Indian income pyramid

Entire country stratified by NCAER-CMCR 2010 annual income data

HH: Household

Figures in Million except Annual Income Strata (which is in Lakh Rupees)

Total Households Stratified: 240 Million

Source: NCAER-CMCR door-to-door survey (2010).

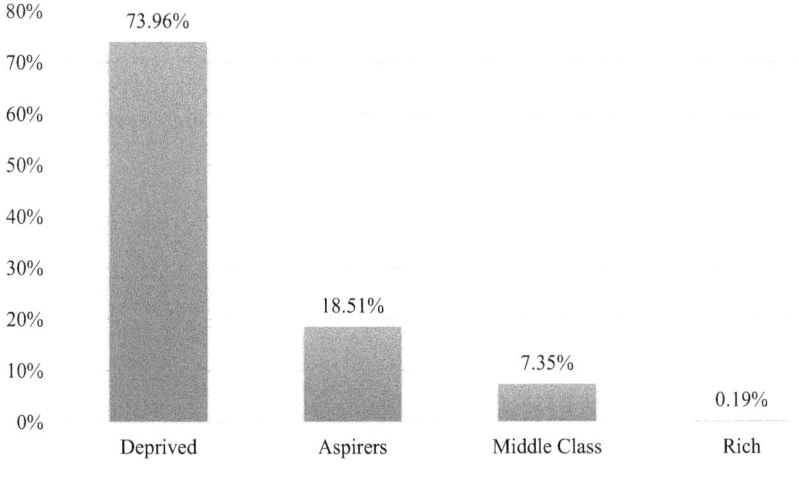

Figure 4.3 IHSD-Round 2 sample disaggregated by household income level (2011)

Source: India Human Development Survey Round 2 Data (2011).

assume that their estimation is more accurate. Therefore, readers must note that since the analysis of this chapter is based on the IHDS Round 2 data, the estimations for the number of people belonging to a deprived household might be overestimated. Since my study is about comparing the number of English speakers and non-English speakers in derived households, this over-estimation should not be a source of limitation.

Tabulation of the number of English speakers in the IHDS Round 2 data-set and sorting them into their household income category produces the results listed in Table 4.1.

As evident in the table, deprived households contain the maximum number of individuals for all three English ability categories. This is expected given that 74% of the entire sample belongs to a deprived household. What is worth noting is that the percentage of non-English speakers in the deprived household category is higher than the average of 74% and is much higher than the percentage of English speakers in the same category. Approximately 81% of non-English speakers live in a household that is deprived, with an annual income of less than £1500. By extension, the household earns a meagre £28.8 per week. The average number of residents in an Indian household, according to the IHDS Round 2 data, is six, thereby implying that each member of the household is given a piecemeal £4.8 a week. In other words, approximately 81% of the non-English-speaking population falls below the $2 per day global poverty line. By comparison, 61% of the individuals with little English-speaking skills and 37% of individuals with fluent English skills belong to a deprived household, which is below the national average of 74%.

From the sample of non-English speakers, approximately 15% belong to an aspiring household. This is below the national average of 18.5%. On the other hand, the percentage of individuals with little English ability belonging to an aspiring household (27%) and fluent English ability belonging to an aspiring household (34%) fall above the national average. This pattern is similar for middle-class and rich households. While only 4% of non-English speakers are a part of a middle-class household, 12% of little speakers and

Table 4.1 Percentage of English speakers segregated by annual household income (2011)

	National Average	*No English*	*Little English*	*Fluent English*
Deprived	73.96	81.16	61.38	37.15
Aspirers	18.51	14.60	26.66	33.75
Middle Class	7.35	4.12	11.73	28.29
Rich	0.19	0.12	0.23	0.81
Total	100.00	100.00	100.00	100.00

Source: India Human Development Survey Round 2 Data (2011).

28% of fluent speakers belong to a middle-class household. Similarly, only 0.12% of non-English speakers belong to a rich household, while 0.81% of fluent speakers are considered rich. Given that the national average of individuals in rich households is 0.19%, the 0.81 figure for fluent English speakers is significant.

The fact that the percentage of non-English speakers belonging to deprived households falls *above* the national average and the percentage of non-English speakers belonging to aspiring, middle-class or rich houses falls *below* the national average – while the figures for English speakers follow the opposite pattern – sheds light on the impact of the language on the inclusivity of the Indian economy. It implies that more than the majority of non-English speakers are deprived and earn piecemeal incomes, while most English speakers (little and fluent) belong to the higher income strata of India.

Further evidence of this income class divides between English and non-English speakers are given in Figure 4.4. 78% of individuals in deprived households are indeed non-English speakers. On the other hand, a meagre 3% of individuals in deprived households are fluent English speakers.

Having established that the majority of non-English speakers belong to deprived households, let us estimate the probability of a non-English speaker

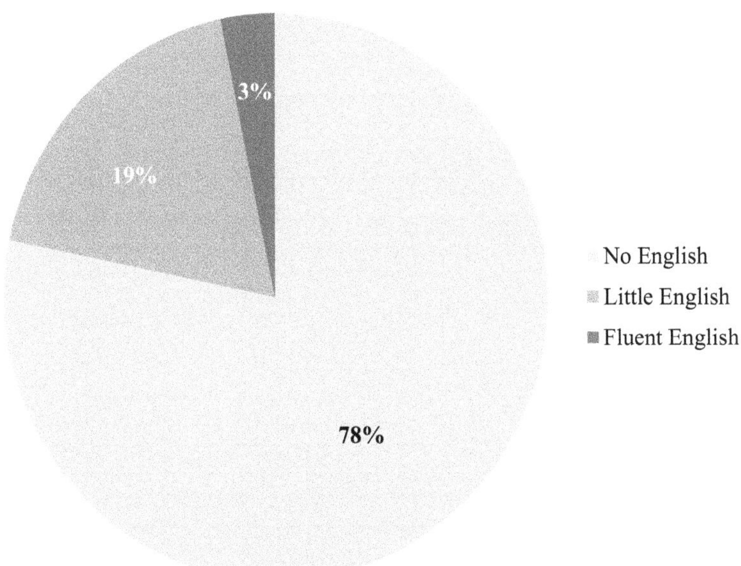

Figure 4.4 Percentage of individuals in deprived households segregated by English ability (2011)

Source: India Human Development Survey Round 2 Data (2011).

moving out of the deprived strata relative to an English speaker. In order to do so, I modify Equation 2 presented in Chapter 3 of this book by changing the dependent variable to a dummy containing responses for whether an individual's household income was more than INR 1.5 lakh per annum in the year 2011.[13] The modified equation is:

$$Income \geq 1.5lakh = \propto_r + \beta English_i + \gamma schooling_i + \delta Ability_i + \varphi Urban_i + \pi X_i + \varepsilon_i \quad (7)$$

where $Income \geq 1.5lakh$ is a dummy variable of whether an individual lives in a household with minimum annual income of INR 1.5lakh or not, $\propto_r$ is the state or district fixed effect, $English_i$ is the response to whether individual i can speak in English or not, $Schooling_i$ is years of schooling completed by individual i, $Ability_i$ is the proxy for ability (including SSLC exam performance, and failing or repeating a grade) and $Urban_i$ is whether individual i lives in an urban area. I estimate Equation 7 with probit to obtain the results listed in Table 4.2.

Table 4.2 Regression of English ability on the probability of moving out of deprivation

	Coefficient	*Robust Standard Errors*
Fluent English	**0.334*****	0.0002
Little English	**0.116*****	0.0003
Age	0.011***	0.0000
Age-Squared	0.000**	0.0000
Female	0.111***	0.0001
Caste: Other Backward Castes (OBC)	-0.130***	0.0001
Caste: Scheduled Castes (SC)	-0.239***	0.0002
Caste: Scheduled Tribes (ST)	-0.321***	0.0004
Caste: Other Castes	-0.125***	0.0005
Religion: Muslim	-0.139***	0.0002
Religion: Christian	-0.078***	0.0005
Religion: Sikh	0.138***	0.0007
Religion: Buddhist	-0.165***	0.0008
Religion: Jain	-0.012***	0.0011
Religion: Tribal	-0.185***	0.0011
Religion: Others	-0.287***	0.0024
Religion: None	0.733***	0.0035
Years of Schooling Completed: 1	0.070***	0.0014
Years of Schooling Completed: 2	0.221***	0.0010
Years of Schooling Completed: 3	0.220***	0.0010
Years of Schooling Completed: 4	0.287***	0.0010
Years of Schooling Completed: 5 (Primary School Completion)	0.324***	0.0009

(*Continued*)

	Coefficient	*Robust Standard Errors*
Years of Schooling Completed: 6	0.344***	0.0010
Years of Schooling Completed: 7	0.407***	0.0009
Years of Schooling Completed: 8 (Middle School Completion)	0.465***	0.0009
Years of Schooling Completed: 9	0.552***	0.0009
Years of Schooling Completed: 10 (Secondary School Completion)	0.681***	0.0011
Years of Schooling Completed: 11	0.643***	0.0011
Years of Schooling Completed: 12 (Higher Secondary School Completion)	0.847***	0.0011
Years of Schooling Completed: 13	0.828***	0.0012
Years of Schooling Completed: 14	0.826***	0.0011
Years of Schooling Completed: 15 (Bachelor's Degree)	1.063***	0.0011
Years of Schooling Completed: 16 (Above Bachelor's Degree)	1.260***	0.0011
Urban Residence	0.320***	0.0002
SSLC Exam Performance: Class I	0.080***	0.0006
SSLC Exam Performance: Class II	0.028***	0.0006
SSLC Exam Performance: Class III	-0.047***	0.0006
Has Repeated/ Failed a Grade	-0.132***	0.0002
District Fixed Effects	Yes	
Number of Observations (weighted)	499,704,821	

Notes: The sample consists of individuals, both male and female, aged 18–65 who reported wage and salary work (34,335 observations in Column 6, with all the comprehensive controls) in India Human Development Survey-Round 2 (2011). The omitted caste group is Higher Caste. The omitted religion dummy is Hindu. The omitted educational attainment group is zero years of schooling completed. The omitted dummy for SSLC exam performance is those who reported valid blank i.e. did not give the SSLC exam (there were a few values not pertaining to any sub-category that needed to be cleaned or dropped). Asterisk denotes significance level (= 10%, ** = 5% and *** = 1%). Robust Standard Errors are shown in parentheses.*

The likelihood of fluent English speakers moving out of the deprived income strata by earning INR 1.5 lakh or more is 33.4% higher than that of non-English speakers. Even individuals who speak little English are on an average 11.6% more likely to leave this low-income group relative to individuals who speak no English.

It is worth noting that the ability to speak fluent English is more likely to enable an individual to move out of the deprived income strata than never failing an exam or getting a first division in a secondary school exam. Individuals without English language ability are therefore disadvantaged, as they not only belong predominantly to the deprived income strata, but they are also least likely to upgrade from this stratum relative to English speakers.

Case Study

Anil, a 34 year old man from a village in Jharkhand, works as a personal driver to a family in New Delhi. He studied through class 8 in a government school and decided to drop out to migrate to an urban area – "my father was a farmer. I knew I did not want to get into agriculture because the money is less. I decided to come to Delhi in search for a job." At the age of 14, he started working as an errand boy for a household, and he started to learn how to drive. By the age of 19, he was a driver by profession.

Upon being asked whether this is the profession for which he dropped out of school, he laughs and says in Hindi "No one dreams to become a driver, but I also knew that even if I stayed in school, my future was either in the fields or in a petty shop. I know everyone thinks that education is important. I think education isn't important, English is. If I wasn't in a Hindi-medium government school, I wouldn't have dropped out. Even today, I sometimes think of going to UAE – they want labour and drivers there. But because I don't know English, how can I even begin to fill forms? Even within the occupation of a driver, I would have earned better if I knew English."

Employability of non-English speakers

A housekeeping room attendant's conversation with a guest is limited to wishing them "Good Morning" or having to answer questions such as "Could you clean my room at 3pm today?" in monosyllables. So we don't expect back-office staff to know fluent English, but that lack of English skill is surely reflected in their salaries. For front-of-house, English language is a criterion to get employed.

– (Group Head of a Hospitality Company, 2016)

The nationally representative data reflects that the non-English speakers are greatly disadvantaged in the labour market of India, as they earn eminently lesser than English-speaking workers do. The conceptualised language-inclusivity framework – Ratio Theory – provides a possible reasoning for this disadvantage – English is a prominent medium of absorption of knowledge in a society where only a small fraction of the population has the language ability. While English may not be a necessity in an economy driven by agriculture or manufacturing, it indeed is an explicit form of knowledge in a service-driven economy like India, thereby disadvantaging those without this skill.

While this conceptual reasoning is theoretically sensible, it is important to investigate whether it is a reality in practice. In order to do so, I conducted semi-structured interviews with 15 elites who are CEOs, chairpersons or high-ranking workers in their services-based companies. For the sake of anonymity, the names of the interviewees have been redacted.

The sub-services within the service sector that I concentrated on were the seven credited for 41% of India's GDP in 1999–2000 and 45.7% of India's GDP, on an average, for the 2000–2010 time-period.[14] These include trade, hotels and restaurants, transport and storage, communication (IT and telecommunication), banking and insurance, real estate and business services, and public administration and defence. The focus of the interviews was on a) the relationship between the English language and employment, and b) the relationship between the English language and wages within these firms. I present a deep-dive into two of the aforementioned seven sub-sectors, specifically trade in services, and hotels and restaurants, in the following sections.

Trade in services

Trade in services, on an average, constituted a whopping 14.3% of India's GDP from 2000 to 2010, which is the largest contribution made by any sub-sector.[15] Interviewees attributed the dominance of the trades in services, rather than goods, as a driver of growth to both demand and supply. The supply for trade in services is higher than in goods in India due to the stringent land laws, labour laws and concentration of capital that exist in the country, thereby making manufacturing a field with major barriers to entrepreneurship. Consequently, most small and medium enterprises and start-ups find it more convenient to pursue trade in services rather than goods. The increase in the demand for trade in services has been attributed to the liberalisation of the economy in the 1990s accompanied by increased globalisation and technological advances. This is evidenced by the fact that in fiscal year 2010, 48.5% of the services export of India was in the field of computer and information.[16]

Generally, a good service is one where employees have suitable communication skills in order to gain and retain clients. When that service is within the trade domain, the clients are global ones. For good service delivery in trade, it is therefore mandatory for the employees to have good communication skills in the global language of English so as to please the international consumer base.

The interviewees conceded that though English is a necessary skill for trade in services, most firms in this business do not invest in training their staff in case they lack the ability, as

> English language is a pre-requisite. Firms prefer employing workers who already possess this skill. It is a more efficient option, in terms of both time and cost, than hiring those without the skill and training them. Unlike teaching someone how to use a machine, which can be done in a few hours, teaching someone a new language takes a long time.[17]

This unwillingness of service trade firms to train their staff in a skill they consider necessary embeds further the barrier to employment for non-English speakers.

This barrier to employment, however, does not trickle down the entire supply chain because regardless of the service one is exporting, employment is at the front-office and back-office. The workers in the back-office need not be proficient in English since they communicate with their supervisors and not the clients directly. In this regard, employment opportunities in service trades are available to non-English speakers but with two catches: it is circumscribed to non-client-facing jobs and, axiomatically, it is low paying.

To corroborate these revelations from the qualitative interactions, I use the IHDS Round 2 survey and limit the sample to those individuals who selected occupations pertaining to trade in services. Unfortunately, a clear classification of occupations was not provided, as the IHDS questionnaire permitted an open response to the occupation question. Nonetheless, a weight-assumed sample of 87,746 individuals listed themselves as Managers in Wholesale/Retail Services and 2,281,877 individuals listed themselves as Assemblers, thereby making it possible for me to analyse the wages and English-skills of a client-facing worker relative to a back-office worker. It must be noted that those listed as assemblers do not necessarily solely belong to the wholesale/retail sub-sector, and there is no way to differentiate them in the dataset. Nevertheless, since wholesale/retail assemblers are a subset of the group, one could get a reasonable idea of their standing in the sub-sector (see Table 4.3).

Substantiating the opinions presented in the interviews, the data reflects that only 13.25% of managers in wholesale and retail do not know English, while they earn an average annual wage of INR 1.5 lakh (£1500), thereby falling in the "aspirers" income strata. On the other hand, 52.58% of assemblers do not know English, earn an average annual wage of INR 87 thousand (£870) and consequently fall in the "deprived" income strata.

Since the computer and information sector constitutes almost half the service exports in India, I conduct a similar analysis using individuals who listed themselves as "Technology Engineers" and "Printers." Again, readers

Table 4.3 Average annual earnings and percentage of non-English speakers (managers in wholesale/retail versus assemblers)

	Managers in Wholesale/ Retail	*Assemblers*
Average Annual Earnings	INR 152,322	INR 86,822
Percentage of Non-English Speakers	13.25	52.58
Percentage of Little-English Speakers	46.34	43.15
Percentage of Fluent English Speakers	40.41	4.27
Weight-Assumed Observations	87,746	2,281,877

Source: India Human Development Survey Round 2 Data (2011).

Table 4.4 Average annual earnings and percentage of non-English speakers (technology engineers versus printers)

	Technology Engineers	*Printers*
Average Annual Earnings	INR 292,052	INR 63,341
Percentage of Non-English Speakers	7.10	52.76
Percentage of Little-English Speakers	25.00	37.84
Percentage of Fluent English Speakers	67.90	9.41
Weight-Assumed Observations	829,080	136,422

Source: India Human Development Survey Round 2 Data (2011).

must take precaution that all individuals listed in these groups do not necessarily belong in the international trade arena, and our sample of interest is just a subset (see Table 4.4).

As expected, technology engineers are predominantly English speaking, with only 7.10% of the population lacking this language skill. On an average, technology engineers are aspirers earning INR 2.9 lakh (£2,900) annually. In contrast, individuals who listed themselves as printers earn a mere INR 63 thousand (£630) and are mainly non-English speakers. This data corroborates the opinions presented in the interview that trade in services is a favourable sub-sector for English speakers only. Non-English speakers are unfortunately disadvantaged in terms of wages as well as job positioning and professional growth within the sector.

Hotels and restaurants

To understand the relevance of the English language in the hotels and restaurants sub-service, four interviews with representatives from resorts/hotels, spread across boutique to luxury, were conducted. From the qualitative interaction, it becomes evident that, similar to trade in services, the hotels and restaurants sub-sector views the English language with relevance due to their international clientele. Even the Indian clients are generally non-local residents, who might not be familiar with the native language of the location. English becomes the primary language of communication in this industry, and, by extension, an employment criterion. This is substantiated by an interviewee's comment, who stated, "It's a client-facing job. Given that most of our clients speak English, it is absolutely necessary that our staff is well-versed in the language."

The qualitative interactions revealed that English is not only circumscribed as an employment criterion in the hotel and restaurant sector, but it is also a criterion for entering higher positions within firms. Substantiating this are the responses given by all four interviewees to two questions (see Table 4.5) – is English a criterion of employment in the sector and is English a prerequisite for higher paying jobs?

The aforementioned qualitative transcripts reveal that, similar to trade in services, the hotel and restaurant sector puts great emphasis on the English language as a prerequisite for employment and growth within the firm. To deduce the repercussions of this accreditation granted to the language, I use IHDS Round 2 data to estimate average annual income and the percentage of English-speakers in managerial positions vis-à-vis back-office positions in the said sector. The results are provided in Table 4.6.

As anticipated, the managerial positions are mostly populated with English speakers, with non-English speakers occupying approximately 27% of the posts. The back-end positions, on the other hand, are populated with non-English speakers who constitute about 65% of the sample. Additionally, those in managerial positions earn three times more than those in back-end positions, with the average income of the latter falling within the "deprived" domain. Thus, in coherence with the findings in the trade in services sector, the hotel and restaurant domain also grants substantial returns, both in terms of employability and higher wages, to those that speak in English.

From the interviews across all the seven sub-sectors, it became evident that these individuals of high postings construed the term "employment" to be circumscribed to job posts with medium to high salaries, which is only offered to English speakers. On being prompted further about employment opportunities for non-English speakers, they revealed that while employment opportunities do exist for people lacking this language ability, these opportunities are circumscribed to clerical and low-wage jobs.[18] They predominantly take on the roles of drivers, cleaners, clerks, security guards and so on because these firms follow a strict criterion of mainly employing English speakers in the client-facing, high wage positions. Overall, from the interviews two conclusions emerged: first, non-English speakers are less likely to get employed in the growth driving service sector; and second, non-English speakers who do get employed in the service sector are predominantly in low-paying occupations.

Table 4.5 Qualitative responses pertaining to the importance of English language as a criterion of employment and higher postings

Position and Company	*Is English language proficiency necessary to get employed in the Hotel and Restaurant sector of India?*
General Manager at a Resort	"*Yes, English proficiency is necessary. The language is important as it is the universal medium of communication. Without it there would be a communication barrier between customer and employee.*"
Group Head of a Hospitality Company	"*With so many international travellers and hotel chains having entered the country, the language is given extreme importance since India is no longer a destination where guests would accept having to communicate with a non-English-speaking member of staff. This has now become a prerequisite for the international traveller – not just in India but across the globe. The other reason I find is that India is trying hard to be recognised as a global player across all sectors and for that to happen, having staff who speak good English is of prime importance and plays a major role in creating a lasting impression on the customer.*"
Duty Manager at a Luxury Hotel	"*Yes, English proficiency is necessary. In upscale hotels like ours, 90% clientele is from overseas. Today we are living in a global environment. If we have to serve foreigners, we must be able to communicate with them and put them at ease. So that is the reason for the importance attributed to English.*"
Duty Manager at a Luxury Hotel	"*Yes, English is necessary, particularly in areas where there is direct contact with the clients. English is given importance so as to draw out a higher calibre of services through better interactions with the customers.*"
Position and Company	*Is English language proficiency a criterion for employment for higher and better positions of the Hotel/Restaurant?*
General Manager at a Resort	"*English, indeed, plays a very important role when employment to the higher positions of the hotel is in question; it is vital for the managers to be in healthy communication with the customers without any barriers.*"
Group Head of a Hospitality Company	"*Yes, without doubt. Senior management must speak, read and write English perfectly well.*"
Duty Manager at a Luxury Hotel	"*Yes, it is an important criterion. I do not think that the HR would like to recruit a non-English-speaking staff in important front-office or senior posts.*"
Duty Manager at a Luxury Hotel	"*Yes, it is a very important criterion. If two individuals have the same skill level in a job, the one having more proficiency in English will have better chances and prospects.*"

Source: Primary data collection for the research – compiled by author.

Table 4.6 Average annual earnings and percentage of non-English speakers (managers versus back-office staff)

	Managers in Services including Hotels and Restaurants	*Back-Office Staff in Hotels and Restaurants*
Average Annual Earnings	INR 250,340	INR 81,391
Percentage of Non-English Speakers	27.48	64.72
Percentage of Little-English Speakers	30.63	26.92
Percentage of Fluent English Speakers	41.89	8.36
Weight-Assumed Observations	368,422	507,750

Source: India Human Development Survey Round 2 Data (2011).

To corroborate the first finding construed from the elite interviews, I use the IHDS Round 2 data to examine the selection into service sector employment explicitly. Specifically, I estimate a modified version of Equation 7 with probit, where the dependent variable is a dummy for being in service sector employment and the sample is all individuals aged 18–65. An individual is coded as being in the service sector if he/she reported as working in a service sector industry. The results are presented in Table 4.7.

Providing substantiation to the conclusions from the elite interviews, I find that non-English speakers are indeed less likely to get employed in the service sector relative to English speakers. Individuals with no English-speaking skills are on an average 14.4% less likely to participate in service sector employment relative to individuals with fluent English skills. The former is also 8.3% less likely to participate in service sector employment relative to individuals with little English-speaking skills.

Not surprisingly, non-English speakers are more likely to participate in manufacturing sector, and the agriculture and allied sector employment. While the likelihood of them working in the manufacturing sector is positive (on an average 4.8% higher than that of fluent English speakers and 2.7% higher than that of little English speakers), it is their likelihood of working in the agriculture and allied sector that is significantly and remarkably large. The probability of non-English speakers working in agricultural and allied jobs is on an average 34.6% higher than the probability of fluent English speakers doing the same. Similarly, non-English speakers are 7.6% more likely to work in the primary sector than little English speakers.

The data thus substantiates the first finding from the elite interviews – there exists a barrier to employment for non-English speakers in the service sector. Axiomatically, non-English speakers are more likely to work in the manufacturing and agricultural sectors. If the Indian economy was driven by the manufacturing sector or the agricultural sector, this barrier to employment in services would not have been a hindrance to inclusive

Table 4.7 Effects of English speaking ability on the probability of sector employment

	Service Sector	*Manufacturing Sector*	*Agriculture and Allied Sector*
Non-English Speakers Relative to Fluent English Speakers	-0.144*** (0.0005)	0.048*** (0.0006)	0.346*** (0.0009)
Non-English Speakers Relative to Little English Speakers	-0.083*** (0.0003)	0.027*** (0.0003)	0.107*** (0.0004)
District Fixed Effects	Yes	Yes	Yes
Pseudo R-Squared	0.16	0.12	0.30
Observations (weighted)	197,511865	191,943,973	186,189,180

Source: India Human Development Survey Round 2 (2011).

Table 4.8 Average annual earnings and percentage of non-English speakers by occupation (service sector)

	Managerial/High Posts	*Labour/Low Posts*
Average Annual Earnings	INR 2,39,238	INR 35,147
Percentage of Non-English Speakers	20.87	84.06
Number of Respondents	417	16,944
Number of Respondents (Weighted)	2,268,916	101,369,556

Source: India Human Development Survey – Round 2 Data (2011).

growth. However, since Indian economic growth is so far service-dependent, non-English speakers are being excluded from the prosperity by being barred from working in the growing sector.

To corroborate the second finding inferred from the elite interviews pertaining to the low posts-low wages standing of non-English speakers within the service sector, I again use the IHDS Round 2 and limit the sample to individuals of ages 18–65 working in the service sector. The richness of the IHDS Round 2 dataset enables me to analyse the occupations of these individuals within the service sector.

I would have ideally preferred to look at occupation classifications individually for the seven aforementioned industries of the service sector. Unfortunately, IHDS Round 2 does not have a clean classification of each individual's position in his or her occupation. Nevertheless, it does contain categories for managerial posts.

As evident from Table 4.8, managerial positions are predominantly occupied by English speakers with only 20.87% of non-English speakers employed in the said tier. On the other hand, non-English speakers, who constitute 84.06% of the low-post labour force, predominantly occupy lower posts. Furthermore, the difference between the average annual earnings of a manager relative to a low-post job is substantial, with the former earning INR 2.39 lakh and the latter earning INR 0.35 lakh.

Case Study

26 year old Padma is originally from Ranikhet, Uttarakhand. She is currently working in a boutique hotel as a housekeeping staff in Chandigarh – "hospitality was something I was always interested in. When I was younger, I wanted to become an airhostess and travel the world – but then I realised that one needs to be able to speak in English to do so. I then decided to work in hotels instead."

Padma's mother – a tailor who was the sole breadwinner of the household during Padma's school going days – encouraged education. "My mother would never let me skip school, even though it was a Hindi-medium school. She always said that education is important and will help me become something. I think she was right – education gave me ambition. But I don't think it gave me the skills to achieve my ambition. I don't know English, which is why, even though I am in the hospitality sector, I work as housekeeping staff. I work in a boutique hotel because the bigger hotels won't even hire housekeepers who can't speak little English."

What are the summarised implications?

This chapter of the book commenced with the revelation that 74% of the nationally representative population of India falls in the deprived strata, earning less than INR 1.5 lakh per annum, thereby falling below the $2 per day global poverty line. Segregation by English proficiency reflects that 81.16% of the non-English-speaking population falls into the deprived strata.

By comparison, 61% of the individuals with little English-speaking skills and 37% of individuals with fluent English skills belong to a deprived household, which is below the national average of 74%. To make matters bleaker, the likelihood of fluent English speakers moving out of the deprived income strata by earning INR 1.5 lakh or more is 33.4% higher than that of non-English speakers. Even individuals who speak little English are on an average 11.6%more likely to leave this low-income group relative to individuals who speak no English.

These results empirically back the notion that non-English speakers are disadvantaged due to India's reliance on the service sector. This reliance results in two disadvantages. First, it causes a barrier to entry into employment for non-English speakers, as individuals with no English-speaking skills are on an average 14.4% less likely to participate in service sector employment relative to individuals with fluent English skills. Second, it acts as a barrier to entry to high-post, high wage jobs, with lower posts predominantly occupied by non-English speakers (who constitute 84.06% of the low-post labour force earning substantially lesser wages relative to English speakers).

The limitation of the results provided in this chapter, however, is that it relies heavily on the IHDS Round 2 data, which was collected in 2011 and published in 2015. At the time, India relied heavily on the service sector. Since then, the Government of India has extensively stressed on the "Make in India" policy that commenced in 2014, whereby efforts are being made to shift India's reliance on services to manufacturing. While the roots of the ongoing "'Make in India" initiative lies in the "National Strategy for Manufacturing" prepared in 2006 by the National Manufacturing Competitiveness Council (NMCC), set up by the United Progressive Alliance government, yet the practical thrust has been realised extensively in recent years.

For instance, defence constituted as one of the seven sub-sectors within services that largely impacted the Indian growth rate. Since the implementation of "Make in India" (and at the time of writing this book), the Defence Acquisition Council, chaired by Mr Arun Jaitely, has cleared defence projects worth INR 80,000 crores.[19] Within the telecommunication domain, Lava, India's fourth largest cell phone maker, is shifting its base from China to India. The company, which sells Lava and Xolo branded phones, plans to spend INR 500 crore in local operations over three years, after which it will shift most or all of its production from China to India. The central government is giving a 25% subsidy and various state governments are offering VAT-free operations, among others.[20]

This altering backdrop would have implications on the demand for labour and impact of wages in the manufacturing as well as service sectors. While the demand for labour force in the former is likely to rise, the demand for those in the latter will face a decline. This would have economic implications on the employability and wage levels of the labour force. The limitation of the results presented in this book, therefore, is that it relies heavily on 2011 data in a backdrop of an altering economic environment. There is a need to pursue a similar study using the latest data figures. However, due to unavailability on English proficiency data, such a study is currently infeasible.

Notes

1 Retrieved from www.mkgandhi.org/towrds_edu/chap02.htm

2 "Subaltern" is a term propagated by Antonio Gramsci (1971) to refer to depressed groups in society that suffer from the hegemony of the ruling class.

3 Sullivan, A. (2002). Bourdieu and education: How useful is Bourdieu's theory for researchers? *The Netherlands' Journal of Social Sciences*, *38*(2), 144–166.
4 *Social Theory Rewired*. (2016). *Power/ knowledge – Michel Foucault*. Retrieved March 16, 2019, from http://routledgesoc.com/category/profile-tags/power knowledge
5 *The Times of India*. (2014, May 20). *Grade system scores for CBSE students*. Retrieved May 23, 2014, from http://timesofindia.indiatimes.com/city/bangalore/Grade-system-scores-for-CBSE-students/articleshow/35356129.cms
6 Anil Swarup, an IAS Officer and former Secretary in the Government of India, famously tweeted this on 19 May 2018 after Prime Minister Narendra Modi's misspelling of the attempted acronym STRENGTH at a delegation level talk.
7 One must note that though the concept of cultural capital fails to theoretically explain India's language-inclusive growth relationship, it can very well and successfully be the theoretical rationale for the language-inclusive growth relationship of other countries. This study is in no way implying that the cultural capital concept is a universal empirical failure.
8 Lee, English language and economic growth: Cross-country empirical evidence.
9 Hope, N., Kochar, A., Noll, R., and Srinivasan, T. N. (2013). *Economic reform in India: Challenges, prospects, and lessons*. New York: Cambridge University Press.
10 Coleman, *The English language in development*.
11 Lamb, M., and Coleman, H. (2008). Literacy in English and the transformation of self and society in post-Soeharto Indonesia. *International Journal of Bilingual Education and Bilingualism*, *11*(2), 189–205.
12 *The New York Times*, India faces a linguistic truth: English spoken here.
13 An individual was coded as 1 if he/she had an annual household income of INR 1.5 lakh and above, and 0 otherwise.
14 Refer to Table 2.3 for the breakdown of the sub-services' share of GDP in India.
15 Mukherjee, *The service sector in India*.
16 Ibid.
17 Qualitative finding revealed during primary data collection. The name of the respondent has been kept anonymous as per request.
18 We had established in Chapter 3 of the book that fluent English speakers on average earn 28% more than non-English speakers in the service sector. However, that finding does not do justice in explaining the degree of disadvantage faced by non-English speakers. After all, an individual could earn 28% less than a billionaire and still be rich with a luxurious standard of living.
19 *The Indian Express*. (2014). *Defence projects get Rs 80,000 cr push from govt; six made-in-India submarines also on list*. Retrieved August 23, 2018, from http://indianexpress.com/article/india/india-others/centre-gives-nod-to-defence-projects-worth-rs-80000-cr/
20 *The Economic Times*. (2014, October 27). *Lava to soon shift manufacturing base from China to India*. Retrieved August 23, 2018, from http://economictimes.indiatimes.com/tech/hardware/lava-to-soon-shift-manufacturing-base-from-china-to-india/articleshow/44943590.cms?intenttarget=no

5
THE INDIAN EDUCATION SYSTEM

The role of education in the paradox

The case against English in India is so transparent that one wonders why it needs to be made at all. And, more annoyingly still, one finds oneself making it, and **in** *English.*

– (Badri Raina, 1994)

In Chapter 3, we established that the English language is indeed positively affecting the economic growth of India – the trickle down of which has paved the way for increased income/wage returns to English language proficiency. Chapter 4 highlighted that while playing a positive role in India's growth story, the language is playing a negative role in development measured by inclusivity – thereby creating a dichotomy.

The disparity created and enhanced by the language is indeed worrisome. However, doing away with the language altogether is evidently not a feasible solution – not only because of its intrinsic presence and dominance in the social and economic infrastructure of India but also because of its prominent relevance in the world. As Badri Raina states, though it is harmfully affecting the Indian society by segregating it into the elites and non-elites, the "educated" and "uneducated," the haves and have-nots, yet one finds oneself underlining these negativities *in* English due to our historical and economic connections to the language. Given the eminent relevance of the language, what can Indian policy-makers do to remove the disparity caused by the English language without removing the language itself?

One policy recommendation can be shifting the focus of Indian growth from the service sector to the manufacturing sector. The return to the English language is substantially lower in the manufacturing sector, and the language's effect on state domestic product is only enhanced due to its relationship with physical capital investment. Thus, if India's growth becomes manufacturing driven, as opposed to service driven, a certain degree of disparity caused by the language can be abridged. In this regard, policies such as Invest India 2010, National Manufacturing Policy 2011 and Make in India 2014 can remedy the dichotomy, and academics must pursue further research in this area if and when India's growth shifts to manufacturing driven in the coming years.

In the contemporary situation, however, there is a need to analyse the institution through which English is disseminated because inclusivity of the English language is required for inclusivity of income and growth, which will conceivably resolve the aforementioned dichotomy. Though English skills can be distributed through various streams, the most prominent conduit is the educational institution of the country. In this chapter, therefore, I will focus on evaluating the pedagogy of English language teaching-learning in India.

The school system

V.S. Kumar[1] provides a detailed account of the education system of India. In his work, he highlights that originally, the Indian Constitution made school education a state[2] subject. In other words, the states of India had complete authority on the decision and implementation of education policies. The role of the Government of India at the centre was limited to coordination and deciding on the standards of higher education.

The 1976 amendment to the Constitution edited this and today education comes under the *concurrent list*. In other words, school education policies now fall under the control of the Government of India and are constructed at the national level, though the state governments are given sufficient autonomy in the implementation process. Policies are periodically framed and announced at the national level. The Central Advisory Board of Education (CABE), which was established in 1935, continues to play an essential role in the evolution and monitoring of the educational policies and programmes.

While CABE is responsible for monitoring the policies, a national organisation called the National Council for Educational Research and Training (NCERT) plays a key role in developing new policies and programmes. It is NCERT that is responsible for the preparation of a National Curriculum Framework. Each state has its counterpart called the State Council for Educational Research and Training (SCERT). These bodies are responsible for proposing educational strategies, curricula, pedagogical schemes and evaluation methodologies to the states' departments of education. The SCERTs generally follow guidelines established by the NCERT, but the states have considerable autonomy in implementing the education system.

The Indian school system is divided into four levels – primary, upper primary, high and higher secondary. The approximate age tiers are 6–10 for primary, 11–12 for upper primary, 13–15 for high and 17–18 for higher secondary. The lower primary school is divided into five "standards" or grades, upper primary school into two, high school into three and higher secondary into two. The national board examinations are held in Grade 10 (equivalent to GCSEs) and Grade 12 (equivalent to A-levels/International Baccalaureate). Students are largely required to learn a common curriculum until the end of high school, after which there is space for specialisation in higher secondary (whereby students choose between the three prominent fields of arts, commerce and science). As for languages as academic subjects, students throughout the country have to learn three (namely, English, Hindi and their mother tongue). There are, however, exceptions to this three-language rule. If the student is in a region where Hindi is the mother tongue and or is in some other stream, then he/she can follow a two-language system.

There are mainly three streams in school education in India out of which two are coordinated at the national level. One of these national-level streams, which is also the most popular, is under the Central Board of Secondary Education (CBSE) and was originally meant for children of central government employees who were periodically transferred and may have to move to any place in the country. Established in 1962 under the purview of the Ministry of Human Resource Development (MHRD), Government of India, CBSE currently gives affiliation to both government and private schools. As of 2014, there were 15,167 schools affiliated under CBSE.[3]

A number of "central schools" (the Indian term is Kendriya Vidyalayas) have been constructed for the purpose of meeting the mobile needs of the government employees in all main urban areas in the country, and they follow a common schedule so that a student going from one school to another on a particular day won't see a substantial difference in what is being taught. One subject (social studies, consisting of history, geography and civics) is always taught in Hindi, and other subjects in English, in these schools. Kendriya Vidyalayas (KVs) admit other children also if seats are available. All of them follow textbooks written and published by the NCERT. Being state schools, KVs predominantly have students of urban, yet low socio-economic backgrounds. A large fraction of the students in these KVs are non-English speakers. In addition to these government-run schools, a number of private schools also follow the CBSE syllabus. Though they might follow different teaching schedules, their 10th grade and 12th grade national examination books and curricula are decided by NCERT or SCERT. The students of these private schools are predominantly English-speakers from relatively higher socio-economic backgrounds.

The second central scheme is the Indian Certificate of Secondary Education (ICSE) that falls under the Council of Indian School Certificate Examinations (CISCE) board. The Grade 12 – higher secondary – examination equivalent of ICSE is known as the Indian School Certificate (ISC). It is widely recognised that this curriculum was started as a replacement for the Cambridge School Certificate. The idea was suggested in a conference held in 1952 under the chairmanship of Maulana Abul Kalam Azad, the then

Minister for Education. The main purpose of the conference was to consider replacement of the overseas Cambridge School Certificate Examination with an All India Examination. During the meeting of the Inter-State Board for Anglo-Indian Education in 1956, a proposal was adopted for the setting up of an Indian Council to administer the University of Cambridge, Local Examinations Syndicate's Examination in India and to advise the Syndicate on the best way to adapt its examination to the needs of the country. In December 1967, the Council was registered as a Society under the Societies Registration Act, 1860. The Council was listed in the Delhi School Education Act 1973, as a body conducting public examinations. Now, a noticeable proportion of schools across the country – approximating 1,900 as per the British Council 2014 Report – are affiliated with this stream. All these are private schools and generally cater to children from wealthy families.

Both the CBSE and the ICSE council conduct their own examinations in schools across the country that are affiliated to them at the end of 10 years of schooling (after high school) and again at the end of 12 years (after higher secondary). Admission to the 11th grade is normally based on the performance in this all-India examination.

The third stream in school education in India, which is coordinated at the state level, is the state exam boards. The regulation and supervision of these boards is done by the state apex organisation for secondary and senior secondary education. A proportion of the syllabus in these boards concentrates on imparting knowledge about the respective states. This stream has by far the most schools affiliated with it. The oldest state board is the U.P. Board of High School and Intermediate Education established in 1922 as an autonomous body under the Department of Education. The highest number of schools affiliated with the state boards are in Uttar Pradesh, followed by Madhya Pradesh, Rajasthan, Andhra Pradesh and Maharashtra.[4]

In addition to the schools that are CBSE, ICSE and state boards, there are some exclusive schools providing International Baccalaureate (IB) and A-level (examples include The British School, Pathways World School, G.D. Goenka World School et al.). The Grade 10 secondary examination in these schools is the International General Certificate of Secondary Education (IGCSE). Furthermore, some schools provide students the option to pick between two curricula. Students of these exclusive schools are almost always from the wealthy tier of the society.

At the state level, each state in the country has its own Department of Education that runs its own school system with its own textbooks and evaluation system. As mentioned earlier, the curriculum, pedagogy and evaluation method are largely decided by the SCERT in the state, following the national guidelines prescribed by the NCERT.

Each state has three kinds of schools that follow the state curriculum. The government runs and finances its own schools. The funds for the operations of these schools, referred to as state schools or government schools, are provided by the government – may it be the wages for the staff and teachers, or the cost of the equipment to foster learning. The fees are quite low in such schools. Alternatively, there are privately owned schools with their own land and buildings. Here the fees are high and the management pays the teachers. Such schools mostly cater to the urban middle-class families. The third kind consists of schools that are provided grant-in-aid by the government, though the school was started by a private agency in their own land and buildings. The grant-in-aid is meant to help reduce the fees and make it possible for poor families to send their children. In some states like Kerala, these schools are very similar to government schools since the government pays the teachers and the fees are the same as in government schools.

Theoretical rationale

As evident from the earlier section, India has various types of schools and curricula. I would like to highlight here that V.S. Kumar's analysis provided earlier, though detailed, is largely about the urban education sector. The analysis completely ignores the Hindi-medium or regional language medium schools that exist in villages. These rural school are ones that provide no English-speaking skills whatsoever to their students. On the other hand, in the urban areas, there are elite IB and A-level schools that teach the wealthy tier of society, as well as ICSE schools that serve the middle-income to high-income tiers of the country. The students of these exclusive schools are predominantly English speaking.

The one area of fascination is the CBSE curriculum in the urban areas. With as many as 15,157 schools affiliated with it in 2014, CBSE is indeed the most popular curriculum in the major cities of India. Given the popularity, this chapter of the book focuses on the English language pedagogy within the CBSE domain across government, aided and private schools in Delhi. For feasibility of primary data collection, the study particularly evaluates the pedagogy in three Kendriya Vidyalayas (KVs), three Army Public Schools (APS) and two Delhi Public Schools (DPS). KVs constitute the government schools, while APS and DPS constitute the aided and private schools respectively.

It is common wisdom that the CBSE affiliated state-owned schools in urban areas, including the KVs, have students with relatively lower English-proficiency than the students of the CBSE affiliated private schools, including DPS. Professor Geeta Gandhi Kingdon, Chair of Education and International Development at UCL Institute of Education, postulates the relative efficiency of private schools to the fact that they are accountable to parents who pay their fees.[5] Axiomatically, private schools may have to exert themselves harder to provide good instruction to pupils. However, both KVs as well as DPS sit for the same CBSE national examinations – the syllabus, content and papers are dictated by NCERT. Both state schools as well as private schools fare well in exams, yet the English-speaking capabilities of the students in the former are questionable *a priori*. However, there exists no empirical support in literature to substantiate this commonly assumed claim.

The theoretical reasons behind this hypothesised distinction between English skills and the meritocratic marks achieved can be twofold. First, social studies exams are conducted in Hindi in KVs. This subject requires maximum English skills, relative to science and math, and therefore, excusing the KV students from writing this exam in English is a way of excusing them from learning English.

The second and more important reason is that the NCERT syllabus and CBSE evaluation methodology requires the students to reproduce the contents of the books provided to them in the examinations. The exams mostly contain direct questions that can be answered only through memorisation. And the highest marks are allocated to those who copy word for word from the books. Even the exam for English as an academic subject is conducted and assessed in this manner. This enables non-English speakers to give the correct answer without really understanding what they are learning and writing.

Against this backdrop, I attempt to investigate two hypotheses. First, though the meritocratic average marks of the government managed KVs is as good as the private Delhi Public School, the English skills of the former are limited in comparison. Second, the English proficiency of CBSE students is limited in comparison to those pursuing IB. The reason for the disparity is the pedagogy of the language in the Indian education system.

In this chapter of the book, therefore, I present an analysis of English language pedagogy, with a focus on the method of evaluation, in the CBSE education system of India. Using a main sample of eight schools in Delhi, and a test sample of three schools in Chandigarh and Shimla, this study empirically substantiates the stark contrast between the marks obtained by the students to the actual English language reading and understanding skills. Readers must note that the following analysis is illustrative of a few sampled schools and is not representative, and they must construe it as a snapshot of a larger picture.

Methodology of evaluation

The common explanation adopted in the scholarly world within education to explain the disparities between the meritocratic marks obtained by government schools vis-à-vis private schools is lack of quality or efficiency in the former. Typically, school quality is regressed on inputs into the education process, such as students' characteristics, their home backgrounds, and school and teacher variables.[6]

Scholars including Psacharopoulos (1987),[7] Halsey, Heath and Ridge (1980),[8] Williams and Carpenter (1991)[9] and Govinda and Varghese

(1993)[10] use methods to control for cultural capital (including idiosyncratic pupil characteristics and home backgrounds) and still conclude that in countries as diverse as the UK and India, private school pupils significantly outperform their public-school counterparts. In other words, the quality of education in private schools culminates into better student outcome levels relative to government schools. The reasoning for the outperformance, however, is limited to school and teacher variables for quality education and does not take into account the pedagogy in terms of the method of evaluation used to test students.

Kingdon, in her 1996 work titled "The Quality and Efficiency of Private and Public Education: A Case Study of Urban India," collected data from 928 students of class 8 (13- to 14-year olds) in 30 schools across the different school sectors (government, aided and private) in Uttar Pradesh, India. Her paper measured student achievement by adapting standardised tests of numeracy and literacy prepared for Knight and Sabot (1990) by the Educational Testing Service, Princeton, NJ. The paper concluded that the quality of education is superior in private schools.[11]

What is worth noting in Kingdon's paper is that it was one of the first in the Indian context to explicitly reject public examination scores – which are a convenient measure of student achievement since they are easily available data – as the measure of student learning outcomes. She stated the severe lack of public confidence in exam marks as a reliable guide to students' skill development in India as her reasoning for rejection. However, the reasoning she provides for lack of reliability is mass cheating, leakage of exam papers, tampering with results and other unethical practices that are rife in the examinations of the various exam boards. She does not take into account the problems with the method of evaluation used by CBSE, which could be a source of distorted exam results.

A study that incorporates pedagogy as a quality improver in the Indian context is Banerjee, Cole, Duflo and Linden's 2007 work titled "Remedying Education: Evidence from Two Randomized Experiments in India." Stating that a number of rigorous, randomised evaluations have confirmed that spending more on resources like textbooks, flip charts or additional teachers has no impact on children's test scores, the study evaluated the impact of a remedial education programme and computer-aided learning programme. Their evaluations, conducted in two cities over two years, suggested that both programmes are effective in improving student learning outcomes. The test scores of children whose schools benefited from the remedial education program improved by 0.14 standard deviations in the first year and 0.28 in the second year. Those that took the computer aided programme faced an improvement of 0.36 standard deviations in the first year and by 0.54 standard deviation in the second year.[12] Through this impact evaluation, the scholars highlighted that in order to improve student outcomes in India, the pedagogy and teaching-learning methodology needs adjustments.

However, no explicit reference was made to the evaluation criteria adopted in the Indian education system, thereby leaving a gap in the literature.

From the literature focusing on the Indian education system with a focus on private and government education, it becomes clear that quality is an aspect that is deterring effective student outcomes. While Govinda and Varghese highlight that cultural capital is not a factor behind the relatively poor performance of government schools, and instead school variables need to be considered to improve student outcomes, Kingdon sheds light on the need to use an alternative method of evaluation to test student outcomes. Additionally, Banerjee, Cole, Duflo and Linden propagate the need for alternative pedagogies to disseminate knowledge to improve student results. The three literatures thus highlight the need for an improvement in pedagogy in the Indian education system – both in terms of the method of dissemination of knowledge as well the method of evaluation used to test the disseminated knowledge.

In this section, I use primary case data collected from 367 students affiliated with CBSE in Delhi, Chandigarh and Shimla across government, aided and private schools to evaluate the current situation in the Indian education system pertaining to teaching and learning the English language. I also evaluate the English proficiency of 36 International Baccalaureate affiliated students to enable comparison. While it would have been interesting to sample ICSE affiliated students, the rationale for non-inclusion is twofold: first, CBSE, relative to ICSE, incorporates a more holistic representation encompassing the varying socio-economic backgrounds, thereby becoming the preferred choice; and second, ICSE schools are largely private schools where data collection is less permissible. I have deliberately opted for high performing, urban government and aided CBSE schools (KVs and APS respectively) to substantiate two points: first, the method of dissemination of English knowledge needs to be improved in schools; and second, the method of evaluating the said knowledge needs remedying.

The umbrella evaluation approach is that of Case and Comparison, whereby sampled CBSE school students classify as the Case Sample, and the IB school students form the Comparison Sample. Two tools were used for the evaluation: first, a perception study comprising of a student survey, student focus group discussions (FGDs) and key informant interviews (KIIs) with teachers and head teachers; second, an objective test of English reading and understanding skills.

The former tool aided in investigating the perceptions that students have about the pedagogy of English in their schools. The perception of head teachers and teachers were also accounted for through semi-structured key informant interviews.

The latter tool, which consisted of a test, required each student to read and explain a word and a sentence, and answer a question pertaining to a paragraph, from a **known script** and an **unknown script**. For the case sample, a word, a sentence and a paragraph from their CBSE English textbook (from chapters that were already covered in class) was used as a known script.[13] A word, a sentence and a paragraph from an IB English B syllabus[14] was used as the unknown script. For the comparison sample, the scripts were reversed. The rationale for doing so was to enable quantification so as to empirically prove the theory that though CBSE students are learning English (and other subjects in English) and faring well, they are not really understanding the language and developing the required skills due to the rote learning procedure. This leads to them not developing effective English proficiency. Appendix 8 lists the scripts used for the test, and the mark scheme of the test is provided in Table 5.1.

Comparison between select CBSE private, aided and government schools

A total of 367 CBSE students across Delhi, Chandigarh and Shimla were sampled in the survey. 57.4% of the sample were male, while 42.6% were female. The average age of the sample was 16, with the minimum age

Table 5.1 Mark scheme for student test

Known Script	*Marks*
Read word	1
Explain the meaning of the word	1
Read sentence	1
Explain the meaning of the sentence	1
Read paragraph with maximum of three mistakes	1
(Mistakes include:	
• *Misreading a word (pronunciation errors not included)*	
• *Taking more than 30 seconds to read the next word*	
• *Skipping a word altogether due to inability to read)*	
Answer the examiner's question pertaining to the paragraph	1
Overall known script marks	*6*
Unknown Script	Marks
Read word	1
Explain the meaning of the word	1
Read sentence	1
Explain the meaning of the sentence	1
Read paragraph with maximum of three mistakes	1
(Mistakes include:	
• *Misreading a word (pronunciation errors not included)*	
• *Taking more than 30 seconds to read the next word*	
• *Skipping a word altogether due to inability to read)*	
Answer the examiner's comprehension question pertaining to the paragraph	1
Overall unknown script marks	*6*

Source: Compiled by author.

being 15 and the maximum being 18. The entire sample belonged to Grade 11. The rationale for selecting the said grade was to enable sampling of students grown up enough to be able to communicate effectively in the language they are taught in, while not disrupting their performance in examinations (which is why Grade 12 students were not sampled in; see Figure 5.1).

Across the school management, the sample was distributed relatively equitably, with 32.7% of the students belonging to aided schools, 38.1% belonging to government schools and 29.2% belonging to private schools (see Figure 5.2).

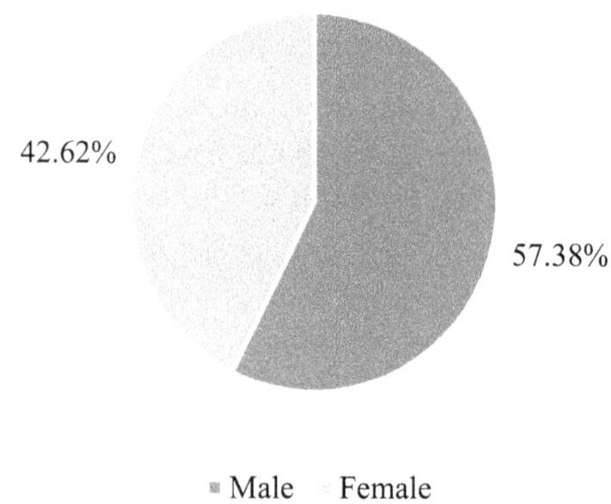

Figure 5.1 Sample profile – gender (CBSE)

Source: Primary data collected for the research.

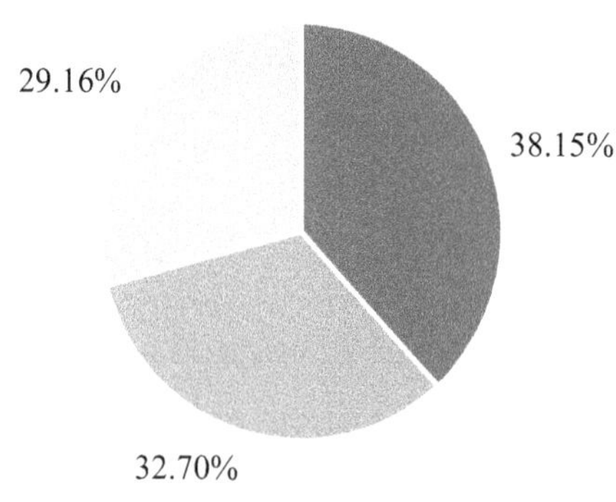

Figure 5.2 Sample profile – school management (CBSE)

Source: Primary data collected for the research.

CBSE student outcomes

I used the marks obtained by the students in their Grade 10 national board examination to get access to the student outcomes prescribed to the sample by CBSE. 34% of the students reported that they scored between the range of 91 to 100 in their Grade 10 national board examinations. This figure is consistent with the 33% of the students who scored within that range in their Grade 10 English board examination (see Table 5.2).

As per the survey results, 64.35% of the CBSE sample stated having received a grade equivalent to A or higher in English,[15] thereby implying high proficiency amongst the students. A mere 1% of the sample stated poor proficiency, with marks equalling 50 or below.

On segregating the overall average score obtained in the Grade 10 board examination by the school management type, we see that the government managed KVs performed better than the aided and private schools. With almost 45% of the sample scoring between 91 to 100 marks, government run KVs substantiated the common notion that the urban school performs well in the CBSE examinations. The private schools averaged a population of approximately 37% who scored in the high mark range. The aided schools' performance was the least effective, with nearly 19% of the sample achieving the highest marks bracket. This data is listed in Table 5.3.

A similar trend is witnessed when one tabulates the marks obtained in the academic subject of English. The government schools had a population of 39% that received 91 marks or above. They outperformed the private schools, which had 37% of the sampled students falling in the said marks bracket, and the aided schools, which had 23% sampled students achieving 91 and above (see Table 5.4).

Evidently, in CBSE examinations, the urban located government schools are outperforming privately run schools, both overall and in English.

Table 5.2 Overall average marks and English marks obtained by CBSE students in Grade 10 board examinations

Marks Range	*Percentage of CBSE Students: Average of All Subjects*	*Percentage of CBSE Students: English Examination*
91–100	34.16%	33.43%
81–90	26.17%	30.92%
71–80	27.27%	23.68%
61–70	10.47%	6.69%
51–60	1.93%	4.18%
40–50	0%	0.84%
Below 40	0%	0.28%

Source: Primary data collected for the research – compiled by author.

Table 5.3 Average overall marks obtained by CBSE students in Grade 10 board examinations segregated by school management

Marks Range	*Government*	*Aided*	*Private*
91–100	44.60%	18.80%	37.38%
81–90	28.06%	23.93%	26.17%
71–80	19.42%	38.46%	25.23%
61–70	5.76%	16.24%	10.28%
51–60	2.16%	2.56%	0.93%
40–50	0%	0%	0%
Below 40	0%	0%	0%

Source: Primary data collected for the research – compiled by author.

Table 5.4 English subject marks obtained by CBSE students in Grade 10 board examinations segregated by school management

Marks Range	*Government*	*Aided*	*Private*
91–100	39.13%	23.28%	37.17%
81–90	34.06%	22.41%	36.19%
71–80	18.12%	34.48%	19.05%
61–70	5.80%	9.48%	4.76%
51–60	2.17%	8.62%	1.90%
40–50	0.72%	0.86%	0.95%
Below 40	0%	0.86%	0%

Source: Primary data collected for the research – compiled by author.

Readers must, however, note that the score for government managed KVs is not representative of all government schools, as KV is generally considered an exception to the norm given its location and central management. Nonetheless, if the CBSE marks are to be taken as a reliable source of student outcomes, then the data suggests that KV students must be more proficient in the language than private school and aided school students.

Self-assessment of English proficiency by CBSE students

In order to corroborate the implications of the CBSE Grade 10 board examination marks, I asked the students their own perceptions of their ability to read, write and express in the English language. If the CBSE results are to be a reliable source of testing student outcomes in terms of language skills, a higher proportion of the government managed KV students should show confidence in their language proficiency. However, data reflects that KV students were in fact the least confident in their ability to read, write and express in English (see Figure 5.3).

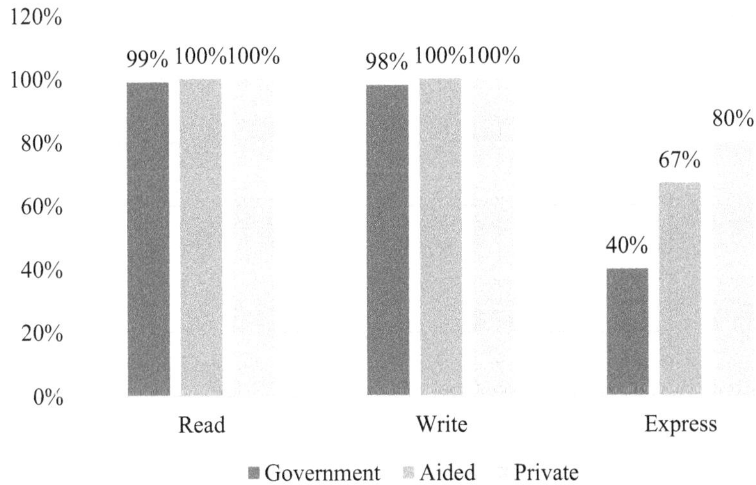

Figure 5.3 Percentage of students stating English proficiency (CBSE)

Source: Primary data collected for the research.

As evident from Figure 5.3, 100% of sampled students from private and aided schools stated confidence in their English writing and reading abilities, while 99% and 98% of the government school students displayed confidence in their reading and writing abilities respectively. In terms of expressing and speaking in English, 80% of private school students and 67% of aided school students displayed confidence. The two managements outperformed government schools, from which merely 40% of the students stated an ability to speak and express in the language. It is interesting that in the management, where approximately 91% of the students received 71 marks or above (equalling a B grade and above) in English, only 40% feel confident in speaking the language. There exists an evident contradiction between the assessment of English ability by CBSE and self-assessment of the proficiency by the students.

Objective assessment of English proficiency

In order to further assess the contradictory revelations of the national board marks and the self-assessments, I conducted an objective English test with all 367 students across the three managements. The methodology of testing was based on the ASER methodology for testing reading skills. Additionally, I added an element of comprehension to the test. The testing methodology has been elaborated previously in this section. Table 5.5 provides the percentage of students who displayed the reading and understanding ability of the **known** as well as **unknown** script.

Table 5.5 Percentage of CBSE students with reading and comprehension skills

Known Script								
	Word		*Sentence*		*Paragraph*		*Average*	
	Read (a)	*Comprehend (b)*	*Read (c)*	*Comprehend (d)*	*Read (e)*	*Comprehend (f)*	*Read (a+c+e)/3*	*Comprehend (b+d+f)/3*
Private	100%	100%	97%	86%	93%	90%	97%	92%
Aided	92%	88%	89%	86%	84%	88%	88%	87%
Government	84%	78%	71%	77%	65%	82%	73%	79%
Unknown Script								
	Word		*Sentence*		*Paragraph*		*Average*	
	Read (a)	*Comprehend (b)*	*Read (c)*	*Comprehend (d)*	*Read (e)*	*Comprehend (f)*	*Read (a+c+e)/3*	*Comprehend (b+d+f)/3*
Private	96%	92%	92%	83%	92%	80%	93%	85%
Aided	89%	72%	76%	63%	69%	65%	78%	67%
Government	83%	64%	66%	52%	54%	54%	68%	57%

Source: Primary data collected for the research – compiled by author.

As per the data tabulation, 97% of private school students were able to effectively read the known script on average, vis-à-vis 88% and 73% of aided and government school students respectively. The trend was familiar in the comprehension of the known script, with private school students leading by 5% and 14% relative to aided and government school students respectively.

What is noteworthy, however, is the fall in reading and comprehension skills across all managements when provided with an unknown script. Only 57% of the government school students were able to comprehend the unknown script. This constitutes a 22% drop when compared to those that were able to comprehend the known script (79%). Similarly, the proportion of aided school students who could comprehend the unknown script fell by 20%, from 87% to 67%. The drop was less severe in the private school domain (7%), whereby the percentage of students who could comprehend the unknown script was 87% and the percentage who could comprehend the known script was 92%.

This objective assessment feeds into and corroborates the self-assessment of the students, and contradicts the CBSE assessment results. The implication is that though KV students are earning higher meritocratic marks in examinations, they are not learning the language in an essential manner. As quantified in the previous chapters, lack of English-speaking skills paves way for lack of prosperity from growth, low wages and low employability. One can, consequently and by extension, construe the reasoning for the low wages and job opportunities available to government school students.

While the factors responsible for the low comprehension and speaking skills of government school students are manifold, including socio-economic indicators and cultural capital, it is the false notion that the CBSE evaluation paves way for that is truly problematic. By using a flawed system of evaluation and pedagogy based on rote learning, the education system provides the marks needed but not the skill that is required in the long run.

Comparison between international baccalaureate and CBSE curricula

The case sample is maintained with the 367 CBSE students. The comparison IB sample constitutes 10% of the case, i.e. 36 students. While this is a relatively small sample, yet – given that the study is limited to comparison and does not extend to attribution – the size suffices as a snapshot. Of the 36 students sampled, 72.22% were male, while 27.78% were female. All the students belonged to Grade 11 of a privately managed school.

The assessment of the cognitive marks obtained by the students in the Grade 10 board exam i.e. IGCSE,[16] shows that approximately 36% of

Table 5.6 Overall average marks and English marks obtained by IB students in Grade 10 IGCSE examinations

Marks Range	*Percentage of IB Students: Average of All Subjects*	*Percentage of IB Students: English Examination*
91–100	36.11%	20.00%
81–90	22.22%	25.71%
71–80	27.78%	40.00%
61–70	11.11%	11.43%
51–60	0%	0%
40–50	0%	0%
Below 40	2.78%	2.86%

Source: Primary data collected for the research – compiled by author.

the students reported that they received scores ranging from 91 to 100. However, only 20% stated that they received the high grades in English examinations. When one compares the proportion of IB students receiving grade A and above in English (46.71%) with the proportion of CBSE students achieving the same grade (64.35%), one can construe that the latter is performing better in the subject. By extension, CBSE students should be more proficient in the language relative to IB students due to a higher proportion of the students performing well in the subject (see Table 5.6).

Self-assessment of English proficiency

As per the marks obtained in the Grade 10 board examinations, CBSE students outperformed IB students. Nonetheless, when asked about their self-assessment of their English skills, the latter revealed more confidence in their English reading, writing and speaking abilities. As the following graph presents, 100% of the IB students sampled in the study believed that they could read and write English effectively, and 86% stated high proficiency in English speaking. Similarly, a high proportion of CBSE students assessed themselves as having the ability to read and write effectively (100% and 99% respectively). However, only 61% of students stated having English-speaking proficiency. This revelation goes against the common wisdom, which narrates that if one can effectively read and write in English, one can effectively speak and express in English (see Figure 5.4).

Of the 39% CBSE students stating inability to speak and express effectively in English, 58% belonged to government schools and 27% belonged to aided schools. A mere 15% belonged to privately managed schools, which is consistent with our findings in the previous chapter (see Figure 5.5).

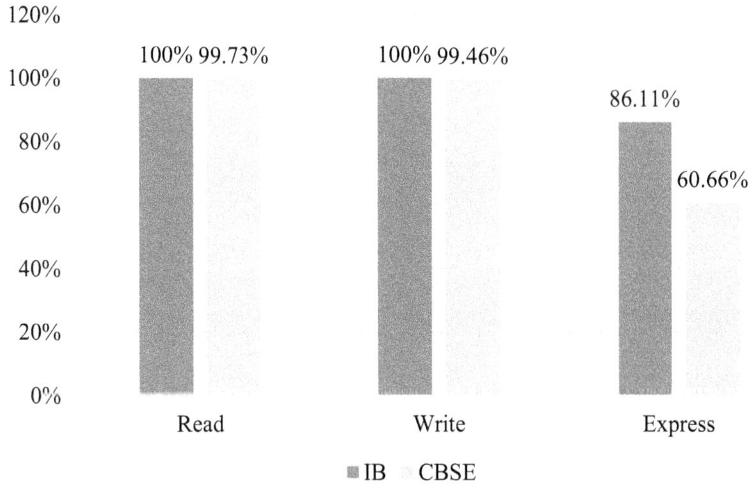

Figure 5.4 Self-assessment of English proficiency

Source: Primary data collected for the research.

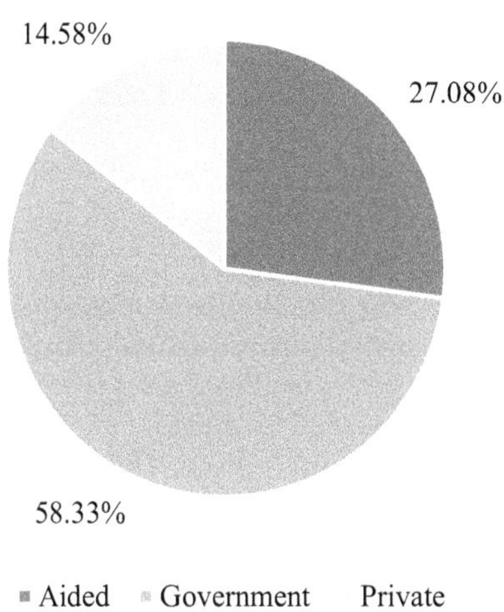

Figure 5.5 School management of CBSE students stating inability to speak and express in English

Source: Primary data collected for the research.

Accordingly, in contradiction to the marks obtained in the national board examinations, the self-assessment by the students revealed that those pursuing IB outperformed those pursuing CBSE, specifically in the speaking and expressing domain.

Objective assessment of English proficiency

To further assess the contradictory revelations of the national board marks and the self-assessments, I conducted an objective English test with all the 367 case and 36 comparison sampled students. Table 5.7 provides the percentage of students who displayed the reading and understanding ability of the **known** script.

As evident from Table 5.7, IB students outperformed the CBSE students. 100% of the IB sample could read the word, sentence and paragraph of the known script. Furthermore, 100% of the sample could understand the meaning of the given sentence and comprehend the correct answer from the given paragraph. Only one student gave an incorrect meaning of the given word. In comparison, 92%, 86% and 81% of CBSE students could read the given word, sentence and paragraph respectively, averaging 86% of the sample with reading proficiency. The same proportion displayed comprehension skills as well. Upon segregating the average CBSE score as per the school management type, one can witness that the reading and comprehension skills were lowest for government school students. 73% of the government school students displayed reading ability of the known script and 79% displayed comprehension skills. Nevertheless, both IB and CBSE students across all management levels achieved marks between 70 and 100, which is equivalent to a B+ and above grade.

However, the assessment of the **unknown script** displayed relatively different results. While IB students demonstrated effective reading and comprehension skills, CBSE students displayed a drop in comprehension as soon as an unfamiliar text was provided to them.

As represented in Table 5.8, on average, 100% of the IB students could read the unknown script and 99% could understand it. On the other hand, only 80% of CBSE students, on average, could read the unknown script. However, only 69% of the CBSE students displayed effective comprehension skills. Within the CBSE domain, while the private school students displayed relatively operative comprehension, government school students displayed a larger inability to both read and understand an unknown script.

The results of the test corroborate the hypothesis that even though CBSE students fare well in their examinations, and thus, performed well in the known script test, they do not completely comprehend the language. This results in an incapacity to express, understand and comprehend any unknown or unfamiliar script.

Table 5.7 Percentage of students with reading and comprehension skills – known script

	Word		*Sentence*		*Paragraph*		*Average*	
	Read (a)	*Comprehend (b)*	*Read (c)*	*Comprehend (d)*	*Read (e)*	*Comprehend (f)*	*Read (a+c+e)/3*	*Comprehend (b+d+f)/3*
IB	100%	97%	100%	100%	100%	100%	**100%**	**99%**
CBSE Average	92%	87%	86%	83%	81%	87%	**86%**	**86%**
CBSE *Private*	100%	100%	97%	86%	93%	90%	97%	92%
CBSE *Aided*	92%	88%	89%	86%	84%	88%	88%	87%
CBSE *Government*	84%	78%	71%	77%	65%	82%	73%	79%

Source: Primary data collected for the research – compiled by author.

Table 5.8 Percentage of students with reading and comprehension skills – unknown script

	Word		*Sentence*		*Paragraph*		*Average*	
	Read (a)	*Comprehend (b)*	*Read (c)*	*Comprehend (d)*	*Read (e)*	*Comprehend (f)*	*Read (a+c+e)/3*	*Comprehend (b+d+f)/3*
IB	100%	100%	100%	100%	100%	100%	**100%**	**99%**
CBSE Average	90%	76%	78%	66%	72%	66%	**80%**	**69%**
CBSE *Private*	96%	92%	92%	83%	92%	80%	93%	85%
CBSE *Aided*	89%	72%	76%	63%	69%	65%	78%	67%
CBSE *Government*	83%	64%	66%	52%	54%	54%	68%	57%

Source: Primary data collected for the research – compiled by author.

Case Study

Fifteen year old Kapil lives in a Jhuggi Jhopar Cluster of Delhi. His father is a drug-abuser who largely stays at home, and his mother is a domestic helper in a nearby colony household. His mother encourages him to attend school, but Kapil prefers to skip classes. Burdened with work, his mother doesn't have the luxury to monitor Kapil's whereabouts.

On being asked about the reason for his reluctance to attend school, Kapil boldly answers, "What's the point? I will end up washing cars for a living like the rest of my cluster men do." Will school not teach him anything that can change his prematurely finalised career trajectory? "Of course not. If I were from a rich family, I would go to a good school and learn English. In my current school, I am surrounded by people like me, who can barely recite A B C D . . . What will I learn in such a school that will help me in my future? I know that even the smartest kid in my class, who gets the highest marks, will end up washing cars for a living. So what's the point?"

Instead of attending school, Kapil works as waiter for a catering company that serves at local weddings – "I end up earning INR 10,000 (approximately £100) in a month. That's a lot of money. I'd rather earn than attend a school that is adding no value." Before I leave, we touch upon the fact that I have met him at a park infamous for being a loitering ground for drug-addicts, and he gives a mischievous smile on being asked whether he is using.

Why is there low comprehension despite high exam results?

Though CBSE students score higher than IB students in the meritocratic examination, a third-party evaluation of their language skills and their own self-assessment shows contradictory results. This finding, though interesting to validate and quantify, did not surprise me. While growing up, I got to experience CBSE, ICSE and IB curricula first-hand (thanks to constant school shifting) and was thus aware of the intrinsic pedagogical and evaluation fallacies in CBSE. Qualitative interactions with students of each curriculum substantiated my understanding – English, in CBSE, is based on rote pedagogy pillaring on regurgitation of content with limited application. Students are required to regurgitate the content of the textbooks in the examinations, thereby memorising scripts, as opposed to truly acquiring a language skill.

Keshav, a 16 year old student enrolled in Grade 11 in a private CBSE school of Delhi, emphatically stated that rote learning is the biggest issue with the curriculum.

> In my school, we have enough space so cramped classroom isn't a problem. I guess, despite all the provisions by the private management, we still question our English skills because we mug up what is in the textbook, and write that in the exam paper. Anything outside of that leads to penalisation and deduction of marks. The main reason I am able to speak in English is because I speak in this language at home, and am privy to a surrounding that is English speaking.

Seventeen year old Safina, enrolled in Grade 11 of a government CBSE school, is not as fortunate in terms of the cultural capital at home. Speaking to me in Hindi, she said,

> English is very important. My mother is a domestic helper, and she always tells me that I should learn English to do well in life. I really try my best in school and can read the chapters of my textbook. I even get good marks. However, I know I still do not speak well. When you spoke to me in English right now, I did not understand what you were saying. I find it extremely difficult to communicate in that language on a day-to-day basis. Beyond what is in my textbook, I do not know.

On being probed about why she thinks this is the case, she smiles and says "I don't know. I do what they ask me to. I learn what is in the book, and write exactly that in the exams."

A CBSE private school alumnus, Sahiba, explains the reason for the lack of comprehension in one word – "*rattafication.*" *Ratta* is the Hindi lingo for rote, followed by the suffix of *fication*. The fact that the act of rote learning has become a noun is testament to the prevalence of it. Yet, to test the representation of the opinions shared during the qualitative interactions, I surveyed the sample of 367 CBSE students about the challenges they face in learning English.

As evident from Table 5.9, contrary to popular belief of cramped classrooms and teachers being the problem in Indian classrooms, the challenge faced by students in learning English is pedagogy and the method of evaluation in the Indian education system. Too much "mugging up" in CBSE and very little application in the course were the top two challenges. 36% of the CBSE sample selected the former, while 34% selected the latter. English is taught as rote learning material, which is reproduced in the examinations. Due to this rote method of teaching-learning and evaluating, students successfully learn the chapters taught in class, but they do not understand the language in its essence.

Table 5.9 Major challenges faced by CBSE students while learning English[17]

Challenges	*Percentage of Students*
Too much mugging up in CBSE English	*36.18%*
Very little application in CBSE English	*33.91%*
Cramped classrooms in school	30.23%
Teacher does not teach the language well	18.35%
My friends/classmates cannot speak in English	17.05%
Insufficient basic facilities in school	13.95%
Cannot afford private tuitions	8.53%
Parents do not motivate me to learn[18]	1.81%

Source: Primary data collected for the research – compiled by author.

It is, accordingly, important for the teaching in the Indian education system to shift from a traditional passive paradigm to an active one, and for the evaluation methodology to shift from a rote analysis to an application analysis. In other words, students should be asked application-based questions in examinations, and they must not be compelled to simply reproduce the content of the textbooks. Furthermore, they should be taught the language and not the art of reproducing rote-learnt content.

The perceptions of the students are substantiated by the key informant interviews conducted with the head teachers and English teachers. A head teacher of a government school stated,

> English is not taught as a language skill. It is taught like a subject in which students have to pass. The only way to pass a CBSE exam is to copy paste the content in the textbook on the exam sheet.

Another head teacher of a government school added that English language pedagogy in CBSE is akin to plagiarism. As a result, "students do not comprehend what they are reading. The simply memorise it."

Head teachers of two other government schools provided further substantiation, equating English pedagogy in CBSE to rote learning with no application. Nevertheless, they did so with a cautionary tone. If English pedagogy were to shift from a traditional behaviourist way of teaching to a social constructivist paradigm, then those belonging to a non-English-speaking background may not be able to get the high marks they are receiving now. A head teacher of a private school in Delhi highlights that there have been efforts by the Union Government to shift to a more application-based pedagogy, substantiating the Continuous and Comprehensive Evaluation (CCE) process of assessment.[19] However, she added that even CCE does not alter the pedagogy that requires rote learning – "that aspect of assessment is still intact."

What can be done?

I stumbled upon a Quora thread online, which asked, "Why do most Indian students like mugging things rather than understanding them well?" The response by Nikhil Kamakamedala that garnered the maximum views stated,

> Rote learning is promoted and encouraged at schools and homes in India. In schools, you might end up getting poor marks if you don't write verbatim from the Textbooks prescribed. When you get poor marks, there is pressure at home. . . . **Indian students do not like mugging. They like to excel. They like to come first. If mugging helps them to achieve that easier, then they wouldn't think twice.**[20]

This response provides the most obvious solution – educators must stop promoting rote learning. For the same, a paradigm shift is required from behaviourist learning to a constructivist approach.

To provide a backdrop, behaviourists believe that "only observable, measurable, outward behaviour is worthy of scientific inquiry"[21] and conclude that "given the right environmental influences, all learners acquire identical understanding and that all students can learn."[22] According to them most human behavior is learned. On the other hand, constructivists view learning as "a search for meaning"[23] and believe that the learners construct knowledge. They propagate that knowledge created, interpreted or recognised by learners themselves, after reconciling new information with their previous knowledge, should be more useful and meaningful. Therefore, a learner's perceptions, memories and other mental structures must be explored to construct knowledge through mediums of activities, inquiries and critical thinking.[24]

In this regard, while a behaviourist will concentrate on the content to be learned and the environment aiding/hindering that learning, a constructivist will concentrate on the learner's construction of knowledge. While a behaviourist paradigm will concentrate on the content in the textbooks that reinforce the student's behaviour/answers, a constructivist paradigm will focus on developing knowledge through active participation of the students in their learning.

CBSE, as it currently stands, has a behaviourist inclination. A prescriptive content is learned and reproduced in the examinations by the students. The scope for construction of knowledge through inquiry-based learning, hypothesis creation and/or critical thinking is circumscribed. The interactions with the sampled CBSE students, presented in the previous section, substantiate that this current paradigm is yielding ineffective results in the English learning context.

IB, on the other hand, falls within the constructivist ambit. With its focus on research and inquiry, and the interplay of asking, doing and thinking, IB urges its students to explore and develop knowledge. The high self-assessment and comprehension results shown by the sampled IB students evidences that constructivism is an effective paradigm for English learning. An alumnus of an IB school in Delhi explains that

> in IB, copying from the textbook is considered plagiarism, and we are penalised for doing so. Additionally, for each subject, including English, we have two-three assessed papers. These range from practical, multiple-choice and theoretical to listening tests. We have to analyse the content of the textbooks, and extract knowledge and meaning out of it. In English literature for instance, we are asked to analyse the poem or prose in front of us, and go beyond the literal. This helps us truly learn, and not just memorise.

An alternative English curricula falling in the constructivist domain, developed closer to home, is that of ICSE. Qualitative interactions with current and former ICSE/ISC students revealed that while the curriculum is traditional behaviorist with regards to most other subjects, its approach to English language and literature is relatively constructivist. As per an alumnus of an ICSE convent school,

> we did rote learn most subjects. However, English is where we had an edge over CBSE. Our English examinations were largely application based, which meant that our teachers encouraged us to apply ourselves through analysis and inquiry in the classrooms.

It appears that, in the Indian context, the traditional behaviorist standard has been reduced to rote methodology. A move from content-dependent method to a content-creation method is required in the English domain. In English classes, rather than focusing on memorising chapters and regurgitating verbatim, we must concentrate on culling out analysis, developing hypotheses and substantiating claims.

The path to the paradigm shift that will discourage rote learning is a two-tiered process. It must start with the restructuring of the evaluation process, which currently focuses on examination papers that promote textbook-verbatim answers, and marking methods that penalise non-verbatim answers. A pedagogical restructuring in the classrooms must follow the evaluation restructuring (see Figure 5.6).

Interactions with the students and teachers of CBSE schools revealed that currently teaching in the classroom is textbook narration based, largely concentrating on content recitation. A student from a private school narrates,

> The teacher usually reads the content of the textbooks in a typical class. At times, so as to involve the students, the teacher makes us read the content out loud. Given that we get marks for remembering the content, the teaching method seems fine.

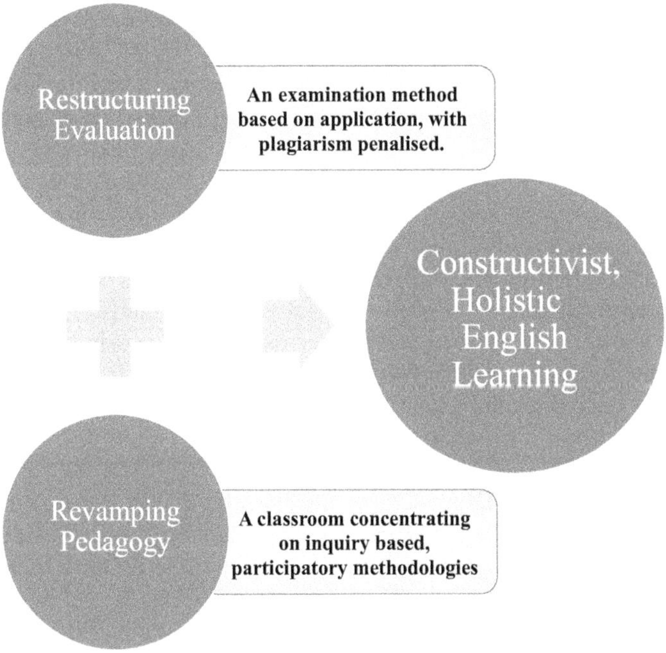

Figure 5.6 Two-tiered process for improved English learning

Source: Compiled by author.

For a holistic shift from rote learning, a pedagogical shift must accompany the evaluation restructuring, whereby the current passive textbook-narration is replaced by more application-based methods.[25]

If CBSE were to shift from this traditional behaviourist way of teaching to a social constructivist paradigm, students would be able to truly comprehend and learn English (as opposed to simply getting high grades without the ability to apply the learning in day to day life). In other words, if the transaction in the classroom and evaluation methodology is changed, and if indirect and open-ended questions are asked in exams so that students are provided an application-based examination (with the examination body leaving space for a degree of subjectivity to encourage independent thinking), then all students will be truly educated. Kerala, being the only state as of now to have shifted to a social constructivist paradigm of education, substantiates how such amendments can increase literacy.[26]

However, one can argue that this alteration will not resolve the problem of inequality of language perpetuating into inequality of income, as India will then fit Bourdieu's cultural capital framework. Children born in and surrounded by a non-English-speaking environment will face a disadvantage in the classroom. Those born in an English-speaking household will subsequently perform better in the examinations due to the engrained language capital. This will ultimately trickle down to disparities in academic marks and subsequently disparities in income levels. Ultimately, there would be an inter-generational continuation of disparity in language and income.

While this may be true, the need to change the status quo cannot be questioned. Rejecting improvements due to the risks that may arise from the reforms would only make way for a complacent and stagnant society, which deters development and growth. Additionally, it is the prerogative of educational institutions to disseminate knowledge equitably – regardless of whether the child is privy to further access to that knowledge outside the school. For instance, not all IB students belong to English-speaking households, and yet the results reflect that they have relatively better comprehension. An IB alumnus revealed,

> I belong to a non-English-speaking household. My father is from Punjab and my mother is from Uttar Pradesh. While dad could speak fluently in English, my mother could not. So we only spoke in Hindi at home. I was in a CBSE school until Class 8, and honestly my English communication was weak. I then joined an IB school, and my grasp of the language increased tenfold. For instance, they told me to take a poem by Eliot, and explain, in my opinion, what the poet was trying to convey – not just with his words, but also with his punctuation use! We were given the playwright Willy Russell's *Educating Rita*, and were asked to enact it to truly comprehend it. We were also shown the film adaptation of it. Such methods encouraged me to communicate and express myself in the very language that the teacher was teaching. Today I am told that I am hyper articulate – I credit my IB education for that.

Such accounts provide reasonable substantiation of the idea that an effective education paradigm can ingrain knowledge effectively, thereby disproving Bourdieu's theory. Additionally, even if the Bourdieu-ian conundrum could be an empirical reality, the first step to make the language more inclusive would be to amend CBSE pedagogy and evaluation so as to enable true learning. The conundrum, and other associated risks, can then be resolved and mitigated through methods such as remedial classes for those that lack the cultural capital and computer-aided learning. A paradigm shift would be a preferable and sustainable option as compared to the status quo. And indeed, a paradigm shift is achievable in the Indian context, as substantiated by the move to activity-based learning in nearly 35,000 government and aided schools of Tamil Nadu (associated with the state board).[27]

Limitation

The foremost limitation of this chapter is the small sample size concentrated solely on North India. It is axiomatically not a complete representation of the country, and readers must read it as a snapshot of the current situation in the select schools of Delhi, Chandigarh and Shimla. I would have ideally preferred incorporating more schools dispersed in various states. However, permissions for data collection in schools was difficult to acquire.

The second limitation stems from the sample size of the comparison IB sample. Since the study concentrated solely on comparison and did not enter into attribution, the relatively small sample size did not hinder the results. Nonetheless, a more elaborate comparison sample could provide a representative, as opposed to illustrative, analysis. In other words, a larger control sample could have enabled an analysis into the *degree* to which pedagogy and evaluation methodologies of the two syllabi (CBSE and IB) affect objective test scores. This could act as an area of future research for scholars.

Additionally, readers must be cognizant that all quantitative data points, barring the objective assessment results, are self-reported by the students. The qualitative data is also the perception of the students and/or teachers. This may result in a bias.

Nonetheless, the chapter provides a glimpse of the larger picture pertaining to education in North India. It would be reasonable to assume that the method of evaluation used (i.e. attributing marks for content copied from textbooks) would remain uniform across all CBSE schools. The findings of this chapter therefore have the potential to hold true even when the sample size and the geography of the study is increased.

Notes

1 Kumar, V. S. (2014). The education system in India. *GNU operating system*. Retrieved May 23, 2017, from www.gnu.org/education/edu-system-india.html
2 India currently has 29 states and seven Union territories. The states have their own elected governments while the Union territories are ruled directly by the Government of India, with the President of India appointing an administrator for each Union territory.
3 British Council. (2014). *Indian school education system*. Retrieved March 16, 2017, from www.britishcouncil.in/sites/default/files/indian_school_education_system_-_an_overview_1.pdf
4 Ibid.
5 Kingdon, G. G. (1996). The quality and efficiency of private and public education: A case study of urban India. *Oxford Bulletin of Economics and Statistics*, *58*(1), 57–82.
6 Ibid.
7 Psacharopoulos, G. (1987) Private versus public schools in developing countries: Evidence from Colombia and Tanzania. *International Journal of Educational Development*, *7*, 59–67.

8 Halsey, A. H., Heath, A., and Ridge, J. (1980). *Origins and destinations: Family, class and education in modern Britain*. Oxford: Clarendon Press.
9 Williams, T., and Carpenter, P. (1991). Private schooling and public achievement in Australia. *International Journal of Educational Research*, *15*, 411–431.
10 Govinda, R., and Varghese, N. V. (1993) *Quality of primary schooling in India: A case study of Madhya Pradesh*. Paris: International Institute for Educational Planning, and New Delhi: National Institute of Educational Planning and Administration (NIEPA).
11 Kingdon, The quality and efficiency of private and public education: A case study of urban India.
12 Banerjee, A. V., Cole, S., Duflo, E., and Linden, L. (2007). *Remedying education: Evidence from two randomized experiments in India*. NBER Working Paper No. 11904.
13 For each CBSE case school, the known script used was different since different schools had covered different chapters during the time of the data collection. Based on the chapter covered, the appropriate script was used for testing. The unknown script was kept uniform across all schools in the case sample.
14 IB segregates its English literature syllabus into A and B. While A syllabus constitutes English as First Language, B constitutes English as Second Language. Axiomatically, English literature B has a relatively easier syllabus and is tailored for those students for whom English is not a native language.
15 Marks ranging between 81 to 100.
16 The Grade 10 secondary level board examination for IB affiliated Pathways World School is IGCSE.
17 The table does not add up to 100% since multiple coding was permitted. In other words, students could select more than one option.
18 It is interesting to note that only 1.81% of the sample stated that parents do not motivate them to learn English, thereby emphasising the importance granted to the language in households.
19 As a part of this new system, student's marks are replaced by grades. The grades are evaluated through a series of curricular and extra-curricular evaluations. The aim is to decrease the workload on the student by means of continuous evaluation by taking a number of small tests throughout the year, in place of a single test at the end of the academic program.
20 Quora. (2013, July 20). *Why do most Indian students mugging things rather than understanding them well*. Retrieved March 11, 2019, from www.quora.com/Why-do-most-Indian-students-like-mugging-things-rather-than-understanding-them-well
21 Bush, G. (2006). Learning about learning: From theories to trends. *Teacher Librarian*, *34*(2), 14–19.
22 Weeger, M. A., and Pacis, D. (2012). *A comparison of two theories of learning – behaviorism and constructivism as applied to face-to-face and online learning*. Retrieved March 11, 2019, from www.g-casa.com/conferences/manila/papers/Weegar.pdf
23 Ibid.
24 Jameela, T. (2017). *A comparative study of behaviouralistic and constructivistic strategy in teaching economics at higher secondary level*. Paper presented at the National Seminar on Economic Education in Indian Schools. Retrieved March 11, 2019, from www.ncert.nic.in/announcements/oth_announcements/pdf_files/jameela_t.pdf
25 The comment on teaching in this chapter is based solely on interactions with students and teachers of select schools. To investigate holistically the

teaching-learning in a CBSE classroom without perception bias, an independent and thorough evaluation of the pedagogy – through observations of lessons – may be conducted.

26 Kumar, *The education system in India*.

27 For a detailed account on how a large-scale pedagogical reform happened in Tamil Nadu, see Bedi, J., and Kingdon, G. (2016). *The political economy of the scale up of the ABL programme in Tamil Nadu*. Retrieved March 11, 2019, from https://assets.publishing.service.gov.uk/media/58db965eed915d06b000004f/Report_3.pdf

6

CONCLUSION

Yes, we have a dichotomy

The way of paradoxes is the way of truth.
– (Oscar Wilde, 1890)

This monograph embarked on a historical analysis and a data analysis of the India Human Development Survey, and it deduced that there were seven reasons for the persistent prevalence of the English language in India. The reasoning included globalisation, US economic supremacy, the historical legacy and elitism of the language in India, the within-country dispersion of English vis-à-vis Hindi, heterogeneity of the indigenous languages, lack of R&D and domestic knowledge generation in India, and the country's dependence on the service sector.

Chapter 3, using IHDS Round 2 data, quantified the impact of the language on wages and household income. It deduced that the returns to English language are positive and statistically significant, with a fluent English speaker earning approximately 34% more than a non-English speaker. When segregated by gender, the nationally representative results highlighted that men who speak fluent English earn approximately 32% more than non-English-speaking men, while women with fluent English-speaking abilities earn approximately 42% higher than those with no language skills.

We also saw that a household with a fluent English-speaking household head has 32.8% more per capita income than a household where the head speaks no English. A further segregation by sector highlighted that a household where the head is employed in the service sector and can speak English fluently earns 25% higher per capita income than a household where the head is in the same sector but does not know English. The effect of English on a household's per capita income was insignificant for the households where the head belonged to the agriculture and allied or manufacturing sectors. This finding substantiated the conceptualised theory that the English language is affecting Indian economic indicators due to the country's reliance on service sector growth.

The third chapter also substantiated the conceptualised positive relationship between the English language and economic growth due to India's growth reliance on services. The quantification of the language's impact on state domestic product reflected that English directly and positively affects the growth in services. Interestingly, it also influences the state growth in manufacturing – the empirical results highlighted that in India, the response of growth to investment in a state is greater the higher the number of English speakers.

Chapter 4 commenced with the revelation that 74% of the nationally representative population fell in the deprived strata, earning less than INR 1.5 lakh per annum, thereby falling below the $2 per day global poverty line. Segregation by English proficiency reflected that 81.16% of the non-English-speaking population fall in the deprived strata. By comparison, 61% of the individuals with little English-speaking skills and 37% of individuals with fluent English skills belong to a deprived household, which is below the national average of 74%.

The chapter deduced that the likelihood of fluent English speakers moving out of the deprived income strata by earning INR 1.5 lakh or more is 33.4% higher than that of non-English speakers. Even individuals who speak little English are, on average, 11.6% more likely to leave this low-income group relative to individuals who speak no English.

The chapter put forth the conceptualised theory and provided the subsequent empirical substantiation to the hypothesis that non-English speakers are disadvantaged due to India's reliance on the service sector. This reliance results in two disadvantages: first, a barrier to entry into employment for non-English speakers, as individuals with no English-speaking skills are on an average 14.4% less likely to participate in service sector employment relative to individuals with fluent English skills; second, as a barrier to entry to high-post, high wage jobs, with lower posts being predominantly occupied by non-English speakers (who constitute 84.06% of the low-post labour force, earning substantially lower wages relative to English speakers).

Chapters 3 and 4 cumulatively substantiate that the English language is in fact causing a dichotomy between economic growth and inclusive growth in India. A possible solution to the paradox is the proposition of making the language, and its learning, more inclusive. There is a need to revise English language pedagogy, which is flawed in two ways – first, the dissemination of the language is through rote learning; and second, the evaluation is limited to the assessment of the rote learnt content. To fix the English channelled growth dichotomy, it is essential that policy-makers focus on shifting from a traditional behaviourist way of teaching to a social constructivist paradigm in the education sector.

The book is the first of its kind in four ways. It is the first to present an analysis of the prevalence of the English language in India despite varying within-country disparity of the language skills. Second, it is the first to empirically back the relationship between the English language and state growth in India. As anticipated, the English language has a statistical and positive association with growth. Third, it is the only research that quantifies the negative impact of not being able to learn the language and its corresponding effect on the inclusive growth of India. It does so by quantifying the probability of the language's impact on moving out of the deprived income strata. Finally, it is the first research into the domain of English language pedagogy in the Indian education system.

By highlighting the seven reasons for the persistent prevalence of the language in the Indian context, my research provides insights into the sustainability of the language – it is here to stay. The research also provides a glimpse into how the dominance of the language is no longer limited to the traditional domains of history, politics and administration but has now in fact entered the economic domain. Thus, the language is here to stay, as long as India relies on the service sector in this era of globalisation. It axiomatically follows that the sustainability of the language could be challenged if India's growth is attributed to R&D and manufacturing.

While technical limitations of each methodology adopted are detailed in each chapter, the limitation of the overall research is that it relies heavily on 2011 data, while India, since 2014, has been making considerable efforts to strengthen its manufacturing sector. It would consequently be ideal to conduct further analysis on this topic as soon as the English proficiency surveys are conducted and published. Nevertheless, despite India's shift to the manufacturing sector, globalisation would still ensure the sustainability of the language – even if the degree of the dependence reduces. The English language is likely to prevail in the Indian context, and Indians must make the language equitable for economic and inclusive growth because, as rightly stated by Anurag Roy,[1] "Indians must not keep their eyes closed in this adventurous period of globalisation."

Note

1 Roy, A. (2013). *Essay on the importance of English language in India*. Retrieved August 23, 2018, from www.importantindia.com/2398/essay-on-importance-of-english-language-in-india/

APPENDICES

Appendix I

Table A1 Timeline of key events of East India Company's annexation of India

1600	The East India Company (then founded as the Company of Merchants of London Trading with the East Indies) was established by a royal charter, which granted it a monopoly over all English trade with the East.
1608	The Company first arrived in India through the port of Surat in the ship *Hector* commanded by William Hawkins. Hawkins impressed the then reigning Mughal emperor, Jahangir, with his grasp of Turkish and ability to drink copious amounts of wine. However, he failed to get an agreement for an English factory in Surat at that point in time, as the port was the most important centre for overseas trade of the Mughal Empire.
1611	The East India Company opened its first factory in India in Masulipatnam on the Coromandal coast of India. The city became a seventeenth-century trading port for British, French and Dutch ships.
1611–1623	The Company established trading posts in Surat, Broach, Ahmedabad and Agra. From the onset of expansion, trade and diplomacy were accompanied by war and control of territory in the areas where factories were set up.
1626	The Company extended its activities further South and established a settlement in Armagaon in order to take advantage of the cheapness of cloth there.
1633	Expanding further East, the Company opened a factory in Orissa.
1639	The Company purchased the village of Madraspatnam, and in 1640 it initiated the construction of the trading post, Fort St George.
1644	Fort St George was established and rapidly grew in importance as a centre for the Company's trading activities in the East, replacing Bantam in 1682 as the headquarters of the eastern trade.
1651	The Company was given permission to trade at Hugly in Bengal. It soon opened factories in Patna, Balasore and Dhaka.

(*Continued*)

Table A1 (Continued)

1744–1753	French and English forces waged a bitter war for control over Indian trade, wealth and territory.
1753	The Treaty of Paris was signed in favour of the British. French factories remained in India, though under British protection and only as centres of trade.
1757	Battle of Plassey – the Company, under Major-General Robert Clive, had a decisive victory over the Nawab of Bengal, Siraj-ud-Dualah, and his French allies. Through this victory, the Company became the supreme master of Bengal and acquired *diwani* (revenue collecting) rights and power to administer civil justice. Puppet governments were instated in various states of India, and the Company got the undisputed right to free trade in Bengal, Bihar and Orissa.
1764	Battle of Buxar – the East India Company, led by General Hector Munro, had a decisive victory over the combined army of Mir Quasim (Nawab of Bengal), Shuja-ud-Duala (Nawab of Awadh), and Shah Alam II (Mughal King). The aftermath of the battle was the Treaty of Allahabad, which secured *diwani* rights for the Company to collect and manage the revenues of almost 100,000 acres of land in the states of West Bengal, Orissa, Bihar, Jharkhand and Uttar Pradesh.
	The Battles of Plassey and Buxar not only secured for the Company a permanent foothold in the rich Bengal, but they also secured the Company political ascendency in large regions of India.
1775–1782	First Anglo-Maratha War that ended with the Treaty of Salbai. Under its terms, the Company retained control of Salsette and Broach. The Marathas also guaranteed that the French would be prohibited from establishing settlements on their territories.
1792	British general, Charles Cornwallis, defeated Tipu Sahib, Sultan of Mysore and the most powerful ruler in South India, which was the main bulwark of resistance to British expansion in the country. Prior to this defeat, there had been two Anglo-Mysore wars (1767–1769 and 1780–1984); both had ended inconclusively.
1803	Second Anglo-Maratha war resulted in the British capture of Delhi.
1835	Civil service jobs in India are opened to Indians. Furthermore, Thomas Babington Macaulay's Minute on Education delivered on 2nd February propagated western education in the country, and English was made the official government and court language.
1849	Sikh army defeated by the British in Amritsar.
1848–1856	Lord Dalhousie adopted a policy known as the "Doctrine of Lapses" to annex Indian native states. According to the doctrine, if a ruler of an Indian state was manifestly incompetent or died without a natural heir, his state would be annexed. As per this policy, around 32 Indian states were annexed (some prior to Lord Dalhousie's governance, as the Company had articulated this policy as early as the 1830s).

1850	The Rig Veda was translated by H.H. Wilson (first holder of Oxford's Boden Chair), in order to "promote the translation of the Scriptures into English, so as to enable his countrymen to proceed in the conversion of the natives of India to the Christian religion."
1853	Sir M. Monier-Williams (1819–99) published an Sanskrit-English Dictionary. His completed Sanskrit-English Dictionary was released in 1899 after three decades of work.
1857	The First Indian Revolution, or the Sepoy Mutiny, ended in a few months with the fall of Delhi and Lucknow.
1858	The Parliament of the United Kingdom passed the Government of India Act. Its provision called for the liquidation of the East India Company and transference of its functions to the British Crown.

Source: Compiled by author.

Appendix II

Table A2 Services sectors included in the 2008 National Industrial Classification

- Wholesale and retail trade; repair of motor vehicles and motorcycles
- Transportation and storage
- Accommodation and food service activities (hotels and restaurants)
- Information and communication
- Financial and insurance activities
- Real estate activities
- Professional, scientific and technical activities
- Administrative and support service activities
- Public administration and defence; compulsory social security
- Education
- Human health and social work activities
- Arts, entertainment and recreation
- Other service activities
- Activities of households as employers; undifferentiated goods and services producing activities of households for personal use
- Activities of extraterritorial organisations and bodies

Source: Extracted from National Industrial Classification, Central Statistical Organisation, Ministry of Statistics and Programme Implementation (MOSPI), Government of India (2008) by Mukherjee (2013).

Appendix III

Table A3 Percentage of English speakers distributed by states (2005)

State ID	*State*	*Percentage of Indians with Fluent English Ability in 2011(1)*	*Percentage of Indians with Little English Ability in 2011(2)*	*Percentage of Indians with No English Ability in 2011 (3)*	*Total Percentage of Indians with English Ability in 2011 (4) = (1)+(2)*
1.	Jammu and Kashmir	7.8	27.5	64.7	**35.3**
2.	Himachal Pradesh	6.6	30.6	62.8	**37.2**
3.	Punjab	4.7	50.1	45.2	**54.8**
4.	Chandigarh	0.4	78.9	20.7	**79.3**
5.	Uttarakhand	4.6	25.4	70.0	**30.0**
6.	Haryana	2.5	19.8	77.7	**22.3**
7.	Delhi	14.5	27.1	58.4	**41.6**
8.	Rajasthan	2.1	14.4	83.5	**16.5**
9.	Uttar Pradesh	3.7	15.2	81.1	**18.9**
10.	Bihar	1.5	12.3	86.2	**13.8**
11.	Sikkim	18.1	35.4	46.5	**53.5**
12.	Arunachal Pradesh	29.1	29.4	41.5	**58.5**
13.	Nagaland	49.7	29.9	20.4	**79.6**
14.	Manipur	7.6	56.7	35.7	**64.3**
15.	Mizoram	11.8	69.4	18.8	**81.2**
16.	Tripura	0	6.2	93.8	**6.2**
17.	Meghalaya	20.5	35.7	43.8	**56.2**
18.	Assam	3.4	27.5	69.1	**30.9**
19.	West Bengal	3.5	9.9	86.6	**13.4**
20.	Jharkhand	2.1	8.9	89.0	**11.0**
21.	Orissa	1.4	8.1	90.5	**9.5**
22.	Chhattisgarh	0.4	7.8	91.8	**8.2**
23.	Madhya Pradesh	0.8	7.8	91.4	**8.6**
24.	Gujarat	2.1	10.9	87.0	**13.0**
25.	Daman and Diu	2.2	15.1	82.7	**17.3**
26.	Dadra and Nagar Haveli	8.7	16.1	75.2	**24.8**
27.	Maharashtra	3.4	20.2	76.4	**23.6**
28.	Andhra Pradesh (including Telangana)	3.0	12.6	84.4	**15.6**
29.	Karnataka	5.2	13.2	81.6	**18.4**
30.	Goa	41.2	42.6	16.2	**83.8**
31.	Lakshadweep	n/a	n/a	n/a	**n/a**
32.	Kerala	6.9	25.4	67.7	**32.3**
33.	Tamil Nadu	7.1	19.8	73.1	**26.9**
34.	Pondicherry	32.0	23.0	45.0	**55.0**
35.	Andaman and Nicobar	n/a	n/a	n/a	**n/a**

Source: India Human Development Survey (2005).

Appendix IV

Descriptive statistics for independent variables

Age: From the independent variables used in Equation 2, *age* is the only continuous variable. I limited the minimum age in the sample to 18 and maximum to 65. The mean age in the sample is 37 years (with a standard deviation of 13.5).

Gender: In the working age sample of 18 to 65, 48.8% of the sample is male and 51.2% is female (see Figure A4.1).

Social Groups: The largest proportion of the sample, approximately 42.1%, belongs to Other Backward Castes, followed by 26.9% belonging to the Higher Castes. The Scheduled Castes and Scheduled Tribes comprised of 21.4% and 8.1% of the sample respectively. The remaining 1.5% classified themselves as belonging to "Other" castes (see Figure A4.2).

Religion: The largest proportion of the working age sample, approximately 82%, reported themselves as Hindus. Muslims constitute 12.3% of the sample. Christians, Sikhs, Buddhists, Jains and Tribal constitute 2.2%, 1.3%, 0.8%, 0.3% and 0.9% of the sample respectively. 0.1% stated as belonging to other religions, while 0.03% responded as belonging to no religion (see Table A4.1).

Years of Schooling: Segregation by the years of completed schooling is presented in Table A4.2. Nearly 30% of the sample has no schooling. 7.4% of the sample has some primary education with one to four years of completed schooling. Primary education constituting five to nine years of schooling has been pursued by 30.8% of the sample, while secondary education constituting ten to 14 years of schooling has been

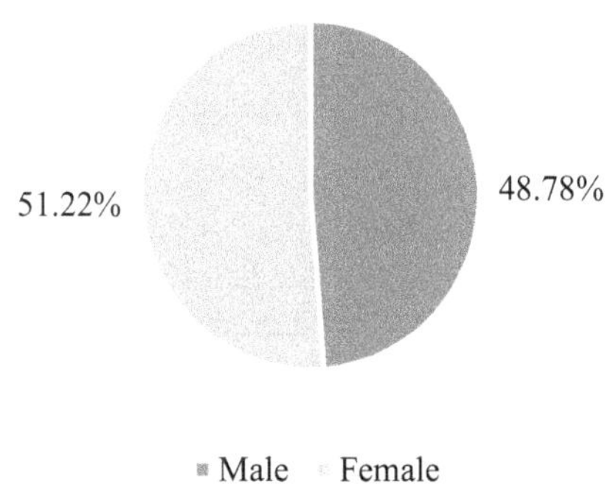

Figure A4.1 Sample profile – gender

Source: India Human Development Survey-Round 2 Data (2011).

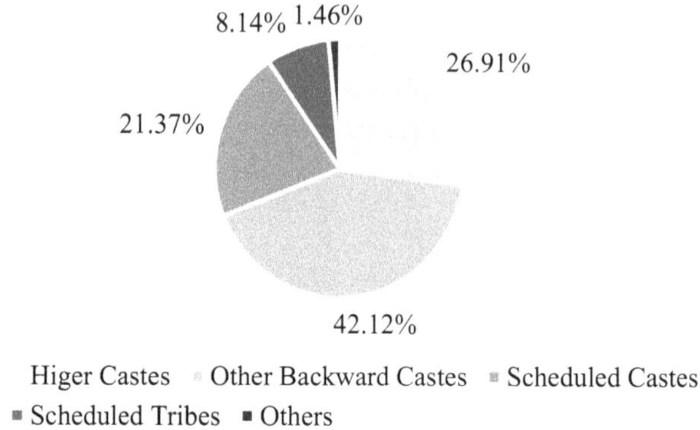

Figure A4.2 Sample profile – social group

Source: India Human Development Survey-Round 2 Data (2011).

Table A4.1 Sample profile – religion

Religion	*Percent of Sample*
Hindu	82.00%
Muslim	12.25%
Christian	2.23%
Sikh	1.33%
Buddhist	0.80%
Jain	0.26%
Tribal	0.97%
Others	0.12%
None	0.03%
Total	100.00%

Source: India Human Development Survey-Round 2 Data (2011).

completed by 23.2% of the sample. Only 8.9% of the respondents have a bachelor's and/or above bachelor's degree.

Urban/ Rural Residence: As presented in Figure A4.3, 66% of the respondents live in rural residence while the remaining 34% live in urban residences.

SSLC Exam Performance: From the sample, 69% respondents reported valid blanks, i.e. they did not give the SSLC exams. The remaining are segregated between the 8.2% who received Class I, 17.7% who received Class II and 4.9% who received Class III. This categorisation is presented in Figure A4.4.

Table A4.2 Sample profile – years of schooling completed

Years of Schooling Completed	*Percent of Sample*
No Completed Schooling	29.91%
Years of Schooling Completed: 0	*29.91%*
Some Primary (1–4 years of schooling)	7.43%
Years of Schooling Completed: 1	*0.42%*
Years of Schooling Completed: 2	*1.68%*
Years of Schooling Completed: 3	*2.16%*
Years of Schooling Completed: 4	*3.17%*
Primary (5–9)	30.82%
Years of Schooling Completed: 5 (Primary School Completion)	*7.77%*
Years of Schooling Completed: 6	*2.57%*
Years of Schooling Completed: 7	*5.03%*
Years of Schooling Completed: 8 (Middle School Completion)	*7.46%*
Years of Schooling Completed: 9	*8.00%*
Secondary (10–14)	23.15%
Years of Schooling Completed: 10 (Secondary School Completion)	*9.89%*
Years of Schooling Completed: 11	*2.48%*
Years of Schooling Completed: 12 (Higher Secondary School Completion)	*7.94%*
Years of Schooling Completed: 13	*1.33%*
Years of Schooling Completed: 14	*1.52%*
College Graduate or Higher	8.69%
Years of Schooling Completed: 15 (Bachelor's Degree)	*5.88%*
Years of Schooling Completed: 16 (Above Bachelor's Degree)	*2.82%*
Total	100.00%

Source: India Human Development Survey-Round 2 Data (2011).

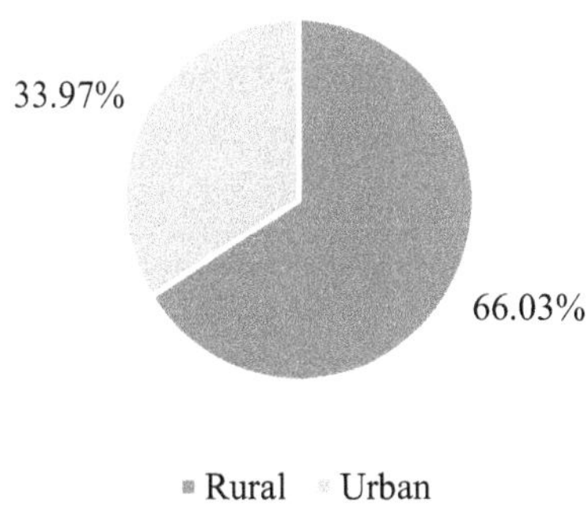

Figure A4.3 Sample profile – residence

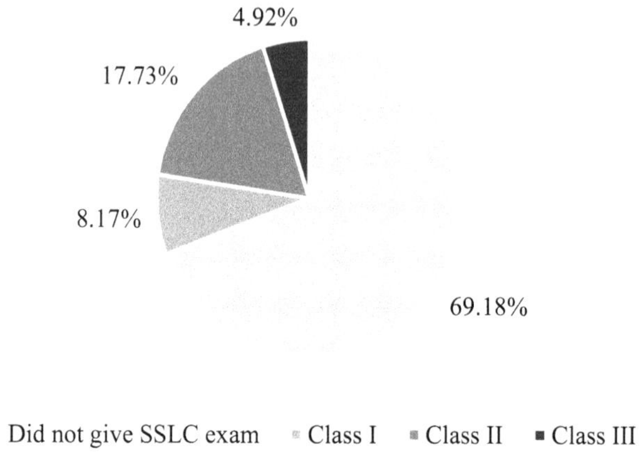

Figure A4.4 Sample profile – SSLC exam performance
Source: India Human Development Survey-Round 2 Data (2011).

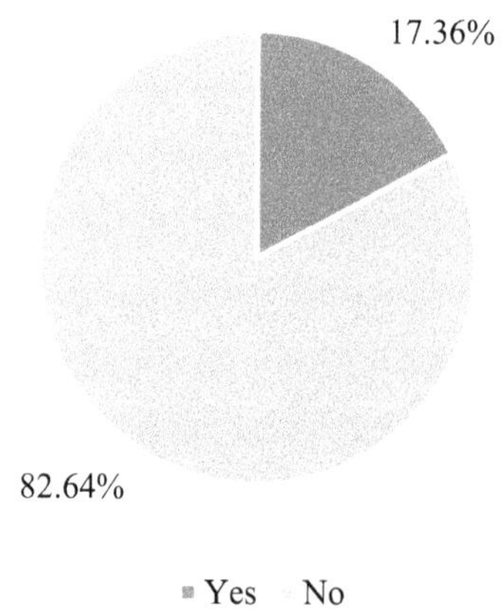

Figure A4.5 Sample profile – failed/repeated a grade
Source: India Human Development Survey-Round 2 Data (2011).

Failed/ Repeated a Grade: Only 70.8% of the working age sample responded to the question pertaining to failed/repeated year in school, thereby reducing the sample to 87,678 respondents. From this limited sample, 82.6% stated that they have never failed or repeated a year. This is presented in Figure A4.5.

Appendix V

Table A5 Returns to English skills on log hourly wages in non-agriculture primary sector by age (2011)

	Ages 18–35		*Ages 36–50*		*Ages 51–65*	
	Household Heads	*All Individuals*	*Household Heads*	*All Individuals*	*Household Heads*	*All Individuals*
Fluent English	3.581**	0.447***	–0.094	0.082	–0.025	0.230
	(0.0876)	(0.3840)	(0.5110)	(0.4365)	(1.526)	(1.2689)
Little English	–0.972	–0.238*	–0.273	0.048	0.417	0.372
	(0.1753)	(0.1406)	(0.3160)	(0.2115)	(0.4324)	(0.3741)
R-Squared	0.999	0.895	0.931	0.883	0.985	0.983
Observations	90	335	189	252	122	127

Source: India Human Development Survey-Round 2 (2011).

Appendix VI

Limitation of the methodology adopted for estimating returns to English language skills

Though the estimation equations (Equations 2 and 3) and the proxies for earnings (wage earning and household income) that I used for this study addressed the main sources of bias, nonetheless there could be concerns about remaining omitted variables, measurement errors and reverse causality. First, it is impossible to rule out that I must have left out some relevant variable that affects earnings. However, for my results to change substantially, the variable should be one that, conditional on all the independent variables included in the equations, has a strong relationship with English skills and earnings. One such variable could be a father's education, which would have been a good proxy for ability. However, it must be noted that although the proxies that I used for ability were significant predictors of wages, their inclusion did not alter the coefficients on English ability much (the coefficient on fluent English variable reduced by 3.4%, and the coefficient on little English variable reduced by 0.1%). Ergo, unobserved variables are unlikely to account for much variation in the estimated returns to English.

Second, measurement error is surely a problem because the measurement for English ability in the IHDS Round 2 data is perception based. It is widely accepted that returns are higher when education and language skills are not self-reported. If this is to hold true, then we can expect that the coefficients on English ability in my study might be downward biased and the returns to objectively tested English ability might actually be higher.

Third, reverse causality might be a source of bias. Is one earning more because he/she knows English, or does one know English because he/she earns more? After all, being in a higher paying job might enable workers to develop better English language skills by providing them with the means to afford English lessons or getting them more exposure to the language in the workplace. If this is the case, then the estimated coefficient of English skills in my study might have exceeded the true return to English skills because it encapsulated the reverse effect as well. One way to correct this reverse causality bias is to consider an instrumental variable (IV) that affects English skills but not earnings. Despite the richness of the IHDS Round 2 dataset, finding a suitable IV was not possible, since every variable that affected English skills affected earnings as well. Therefore, readers should be cautious when taking my estimate for India as reflective of the causal returns to English. Nevertheless, my study does highlight a significantly positive association between English skills and earnings in India, and even without the causal interpretation, the results suggest the importance of language considerations in the economic domain.

Appendix VII

Limitations of the empirical methodology adopted for language-growth relationship

Ideally, I would have preferred to do a time-series analysis using the national-level data on growth in GDP per capita of India as the dependent variable. Such an analysis would have yielded more reliable results, since national-level data of India does not bear the same caveats as state-level data. However, to do a time-series analysis, I would need data on English skills over the time-period of the analysis. Since data on English skills was only available for the years 2005 and 2011, such an analysis was infeasible. I did consider using the national average of TOEFL scores as a proxy for English over the years. However, the changing TOEFL tests over the years made score compilation over the years infeasible.[1] Furthermore, TOEFL would only capture the dimension of quality of English speakers rather than the quantity of English speakers. The IHDS data provides information on both dimensions – the fraction of English speakers as well as their proficiency (fluent or little). Given this circumscription on data on English ability in India, doing a cross-sectional analysis rather than a time-series analysis, was the only practical option.

Within this cross-sectional analysis, the ideal panel data estimation method, which is commonly used for growth estimation across regions, was not used in this study. This is again because of lack of access to long enough data for proportion of English speakers from Indian states. Even for the cross-sectional growth analysis – which is the methodology used in this study – I would have preferred using the Barro-type cross-sectional growth regression model. Such cross-sectional regression captures conditional convergence by introducing the initial GDP per capita in the base period as an independent variable. Controls for human capital and investment are also included. In traditional cross-country growth literature, analyses typically proceed from some form of Barro-type cross-sectional model. The most famous of the growth equations is the one propagated by Ross Levine and David Renelt in their 1992 benchmark study titled *A Sensitivity Analysis of Cross-Country Growth Regressions*. A form of the Levine-Renelt equation is given. $\hat{y}$

$$\hat{y} = \alpha + \beta_1 y_0 + \beta_2\, education + \beta_3\, investment \qquad (6)$$

Where $\hat{y}$ is the growth of GDP per capita over some period, y_0 is the GDP of the initial/ base period, *education* is some human capital proxy in the base period and *investment* is the investment share of GDP over the period. Most cross-sectional studies on growth have used this equation as the base and have then proceeded by adding study-specific characteristics to understand what explained growth in a certain place at a certain period of time. Unfortunately, estimating the earlier equation, with an additional insertion of English as an independent variable, in the context of the Indian states was not possible due to data limitation.

1 As mentioned at the start of this section, my time-period was limited to 2004–2014 because the earliest data for English was only available for 2005.
2 The inconsistencies in the MOSPI data series made compilation of data over longer durations problematic.
3 State-level data on investment was simply not available for India for a longer period. The Capex database is the sole provider of investment-related data since 1995. However, given the database's glaring limitations and the high cost of access, it seemed relatively reasonable to use an alternative method of testing using only the 2004–2005 MOSPI data on GFCF. Given that 2004–2005 was also the base year of my study, I did attempt to incorporate this investment data in the Levine-Renelt equation. However, since the equation requires the investment control to include the *average* investment for the entire time-period of analysis, a single base year data entry proved to be insignificant.

Given these important caveats, a cross-sectional regression based on the Levine-Renelt model was infeasible, as the limitations listed previously would have warranted more than the usual caveat for the subsequent results. Nevertheless, Ahluwalia's work on state growth greatly aided my study by providing a simpler model that is illustrative of Indian state growth, if not representative. This model did not include controls to determine the exact *level* of the effect of the English language on growth, but it did enable an investigation into the *relationship* between the English language and state-level growth.

However, as mentioned earlier in the section, data pertaining to GSDP has inconsistencies and are not completely reliable, as they do not add up to national accounts estimations. Furthermore, the fact that my proxy for English was individual perception of their own English-speaking skills, the proxy was not fully representative of the true English capabilities of each state. These are the two limitations of the study conducted. Nevertheless, despite these caveats we obtained significant observations, which would reasonably get further embedded if we get a good test-based (rather than perception-based) proxy for English in the future.

Appendix VIII

Objective test scripts

ACBSE Script

Word:
Suspicious

Sentence:
The horse stood on its hind legs, snorted and burst into a fury of speed that was the loveliest thing I had ever seen.

Paragraph:
I kicked into the muscles of the horse. Once again it reared and snorted. Then it began to run. I didn't know what to do. Instead of running across the field to the irrigation ditch the horse ran down the road to the vineyard of Dikran Halabian where it began to leap over vines. The horse leaped over seven vines before I fell. Then it continued running.

CBSE Script

Word:
Revolting

Sentence:
She was like the winter landscape in the mountains, an expanse of pure white serenity breathing peace and contentment.

Paragraph:
As the years rolled by my grandmother and I saw less of each other. For some time she continued to wake me up and get me ready for school. When I came back she would ask me what the teacher had taught me. I would tell her English words and little things of western science and learning. . . . This made her unhappy. She could not help me with my lessons. She did not believe in the things they taught at the English school and was distressed that there was no teaching about God and the scriptures.

IB-B Script

Word:
Anguish

Sentence:
Gazing up into the darkness I saw myself as a creature driven by vanity

Paragraph:
Her name sprang to my lips at moments in strange prayers and praises which I myself did not understand. My eyes were often full of tears (I could not tell why) and at times, a flood from my heart seemed to pour itself out into my bosom. I thought little of the future. I did not know whether I would ever speak to her or not or, if I spoke to her, how I could tell her of my confused adoration.

Source: From textbooks of respective curricula.

Note

1 As Lee (2012) stated, TOEFL tests were initially paper-based, with a switch to computer-based testing in 1998. There was a further switch to Internet-based testing in 2005, after which in 2006 computer-based testing was discontinued. Currently, paper-based testing is available on a limited basis to support the Internet-based testing network. However, the maximum score for each test is different (120 for the Internet-based test, 677 for the paper-based test and 300 for the computer-based test), thereby making compilation and comparisons infeasible. Due to this reason, Lee used only the paper-based TOEFL tests for the years 1993 and 1995 in his study and chose to do a cross-sectional analysis.

BIBLIOGRAPHY

Aggarwal, J. C. (2007). *Landmarks in the history of modern Indian education* (6th ed.). New Delhi: Vikas Publishing House Private Limited.

Ahluwalia, M. S. (2002). State-level performance under economic reforms in India. In A. O. Krueger (Ed.), *Economic policy reforms and the Indian economy* (pp. 91–122). Chicago: University of Chicago Press.

All Gov India. (2017). *Department of official language*. Retrieved September 10, 2017, from www.allgov.com/india/departments/ministry-of-home-affairs/department-of-official-language?agencyid=7577

Aghion, P., and Howitt, P. (1992). Model of growth through creative destruction. *Econometrica*, *60*, 323–351.

Agnihotri, R. K., and Khanna, A. L.(1997). *Problematizing English in India*. New Delhi: SAGE Publications.

Azam, M., Chin, A., and Prakash, N. (2011). The returns to English-language skills in India. *Economic Development and Cultural Change*, *61*(2), 335–367.

Ballhatchet, K. A. (1951). The home government and Bentinck's education policy. *Cambridge Historical Journal*, *X*, 224–229.

Bedi, J., and Kingdon, G. (2016). *The political economy of the scale up of the ABL programme in Tamil Nadu*. Retrieved March 11, 2019, from https://assets.publishing.service.gov.uk/media/58db965eed915d06b000004f/Report_3.pdf

Bentinck to Metcalfe. (1829, September 16). *Bentinck papers*. Department of Manuscripts, Nottingham University Library.

Booth, T. (2008). The growing demand for private education in English: A barrier to inclusion? *EENET Newsletter 12*. Retrieved March 11, 2014, from www.eenet.org.uk/resources/eenet_newsletter/news12/page14.php

Bosworth, B., and Collins, S. M. (2007). *Accounting for growth: Comparing China and India*. National Bureau of Economic Research Working Paper no. 12943.

Bosworth, B., Collins, S. M., and Virmani, A. (2007). Sources of growth in the Indian economy. *India Policy Forum*, *3*, 1–50.

Bourdie, P. (1986). *The forms of capital*. Retrieved March 3, 2013, from www.marxists.org/reference/subject/philosophy/works/fr/bourdieu-forms-capital.htm

Bowring, J. (1843). *The works of Jeremy Bentham*. London.

Brass, P. R. (1974). *Language, religion and politics in North India*. Cambridge: Cambridge University Press.

British Council. (2014). *Indian school education system*. Retrieved March 16, 2017, from www.britishcouncil.in/sites/default/files/indian_school_education_system_-_an_overview_1.pdf

British Library. (2014). *Indian national congress*. Retrieved July 15, 2015, from www.bl.uk/reshelp/findhelpregion/asia/india/indianindependence/indiannat/source1/index.html

Bush, G. (2006). Learning about learning: From theories to trends. *Teacher Librarian*, *34*(2), 14–19.

Caselli, F., and Coleman, W. J. (2000). *The world technology frontier*. National Bureau of Economic Research Working Paper no. 7904.

Caselli, F., and Coleman, W. J. (2001). Cross-country technology diffusion: The case of computers. *AEA Papers and Proceedings, American Economic Reviews*, *91*, 328–335.

Chopra, P. N., Puri, B. N., and Das, M. N. (1974). *A social, cultural and economic history of India* (vol. 1). New Delhi: Macmillan.

Coe, D. T., and Helpman, E. (1995). International R&D-spillovers. *European Economic Review*, *39*, 859–887.

Coleman, H. (Ed.). (2007). *Language and development: Africa and beyond*. Addis Ababa: British Council Ethiopia.

Coleman, H. (2011). The English language in development. *MEXTESOL Journal*, *35*(1).

Collet, S. D. (1900). *Life and letters of Raja Ram Mohan Roy*. London.

Columbia University. (2018). *Minute on Education (1835) by Thomas Babington Macaulay*. Retrieved on June 15, 2019, from www.columbia.edu/itc/mealac/pritchett/00generallinks/macaulay/txt_minute_education_1835.html.

Coyle, G. (2013). *Causes and consequences of second language education: A global analysis from 1980 to the present* (UC Riverside Electronic thesis and dissertations).

Crystal, D. (2003). *English as global language*. New York: Cambridge University Press.

Daily, O. (2018, March 21). *13 ways of looking at English: This language gets work done in India*. Retrieved October 29, 2018, from www.dailyo.in/arts/english-language-day-india-obsession-works/story/1/22990.html

Duff to Inglis. (1833, March 1). *Duff papers*. Edinburgh: National Library of Scotland.

Eichengreen, B., and Gupta, P. (2011). *The service sector as India's road to economic growth*. National Bureau of Economic Research Working Paper no. 16757.

Embree, A. T. (1962). *Charles Grant and British rule in India*. London: Allen & Unwin.

Erling, E. (2013, November 8). *The importance of English in South Asia's job market*. British Council. Retrieved January 21, 2014, from http://blog.britishcouncil.org/2013/11/08/the-importance-of-english-in-south-asias-job-market/

Ethnologue. (2018). *Languages of the World*. Retrieved July 14, 2018, from www.ethnologue.com

Ford, S., and Strange, R. (1999). Where do Japanese manufacturing firms invest within Europe, and why? *Transnational Corporations*, *8*(1), 117–140.

Ghosh, S. C. (1995). Bentinck, Macaulay and the introduction of English education in India. *History of Education*, *24*(1), 17–24.

Government of India. (1953). *Report of the secondary education commission*. New Delhi: Ministry of Education.
Govinda, R., and Varghese, N. V. (1993). *Quality of primary schooling in India: A case study of Madhya Pradesh*. Paris: International Institute for Educational Planning, and New Delhi: National Institute of Educational Planning and Administration (NIEPA).
Graddol, D. (2007). *The future of English?* London: The British Council.
Grin, F. (2001). English as economic value: Facts and fallacies. *World Englishes*, *20*(1), 65–78.
Grossmann, G. M., and Helpman, E. (1991). *Innovation and growth in the global economy*. Cambridge, MA: MIT Press.
Halsey, A. H., Heath, A., and Ridge, J. (1980). *Origins and destinations: Family, class and education in modern Britain*. Oxford: Clarendon Press.
Hope, N., Kochar, A., Noll, R., and Srinivasan, T. N. (2013). *Economic reform in India: Challenges, prospects, and lessons*. New York: Cambridge University Press.
Jameela, T. (2017). *A comparative study of behaviouralistic and constructivistic strategy in teaching economics at higher secondary level*. Paper presented at the National Seminar on Economic Education in Indian Schools. Retrieved March 11, 2019, from www.ncert.nic.in/announcements/oth_announcements/pdf_files/jameela_t.pdf
Jones, C. I. (1995). R&D-based models of economic growth. *Journal of Political Economy*, *103*, 759–784.
Joseph, M. (2011). India faces a linguistic truth: English spoken here. *New York Times*. Retrieved October 15, 2013, from www.nytimes.com/2011/02/17/world/asia/17iht-letter17.html?_r=0
Kapur, S., and Chakraborty, T. (2008). *English language premium: Evidence from a policy experiment in India*. Unpublished manuscript. St. Louis: Department of Economics, Washington University.
Keller, W. (2002). Geographic localization of international technology diffusion. *American Economic Review*, *92*, 120–142.
Knight, J. B. and Sabot, R. H. (1990). *Education, productivity and inequality: The East African natural experiment*. Oxford: Oxford University Press for the World Bank.
Kochhar, R. (2008). Seductive orientalism: English education and modern science in colonial India. *Social Scientist*, *36*, 53–57.
Kingdon, G. G. (1996). The quality and efficiency of private and public education: A case study of urban India. *Oxford Bulletin of Economics and Statistics*, *58*(1), 57–82.
Kumar, V. S. (2014). The education system in India. *GNU operating system*. Retrieved May 23, 2014, from www.gnu.org/education/edu-system-india.html
Lamb, M., and Coleman, H. (2008). Literacy in English and the transformation of self and society in post-Soeharto Indonesia. *International Journal of Bilingual Education and Bilingualism*, *11*(2), 189–205.
Lee, C. G. (2012). English language and economic growth: Cross-country empirical evidence. *Journal of Economic and Social Studies*, *2*(1), 5–20.
Library, B. (2014). *The Indian national congress 1885–1985*. Retrieved March 11, 2014, from www.bl.uk/reshelp/findhelpregion/asia/india/indianindependence/indiannat/source1/

Lin, J. Y. (2013, August 5). Long live China's boom. *Project Syndicate*. Retrieved March 11, 2014, from www.project-syndicate.org/commentary/growth-and-the-chinese-economy-s-latecomer-advantage-by-justin-yifu-lin

Mayhew, A. (1926). *The education of India*. London: Faber & Gwyer.

McArthur, T. (1998). *The English languages*. Cambridge: Cambridge University Press.

Mohanty, S. (2000). Language dialectic and Fakir Mohan's rhetoric of progress. In M. Ramanan and P. Sailaja (Eds.), *English and the Indian short story*. New Delhi: Orient Longman Limited.

Moore, M. (2005, November 18). Development's language barrier. *The Guardian*. Retrieved January 21, 2014, from www.theguardian.com/education/2005/nov/18/tefl

Mundy, K. (2006). Education for all and the new development compact. *Review of Education*, *52*, 23–48.

Munshi, K., and Rosenzweig, M. (2006). Traditional institutions meet the modern world: Caste, gender, and schooling choice in a globalizing economy. *American Economic Review*, *96*(4), 1225–1252.

Outhwaite, W., and Turner, S. (2008). *The SAGE handbook of social science methodology*. London: Sage Publications Ltd.

Philips, C. H. (1940). *The East India company, 1784–1834*. Manchester: Hesperides Press.

Philip Powell-Davies for the British Council. (2015). *The social and economic case for developing English skills*. Retrieved October 29, 2018, from www.britishcouncil.org.eg/en/symposium/thought-pieces/social-and-economic-case-developing-english-skills

Psacharopoulos, G. (1987). Private versus public schools in developing countries: Evidence from Colombia and Tanzania. *International Journal of Educational Development*, *7*, 59–67.

Quora. (2013, July 20). *Why do most Indian students mugging things rather than understanding them well*. Retrieved March 11, 2019, from www.quora.com/Why-do-most-Indian-students-like-mugging-things-rather-than-understanding-them-well

Raina, B. (1994). A note on language, and the politics of English in India. In S. Joshi (Ed.), *Rethinking English: Essays in literature, language, history* (pp. 265–297). New Delhi: Oxford University Press.

Romer, P. M. (1990). Endogenous technological change. *Journal of Political Economy*, *98*, S71–S102.

Roy, A. (2013). *Essay on the importance of English language in India*. Retrieved August 23, 2017, from www.importantindia.com/2398/essay-on-importance-of-english-language-in-india/

Singh, K. S. (2008). *People of India*. West Bengal: Anthropological Survey of India.

Sharp, H. (1920). *Selections from educational records: 1781–1839* (Part 1). Calcutta: Government Printing Press.

Social Theory Rewired. (2016). *Power/ knowledge – Michel Foucault*. Retrieved March 16, 2019, from http://routledgesoc.com/category/profile-tags/power knowledge

Spear, T. G. P. (1938). Bentinck and education. *Cambridge Historical Journal*, *VI*, 78–101.

Suárez, S. L. (2005). Does English rule? Language instruction and economic strategies in Singapore, Ireland and Puerto Rico. *Comparative Politics*, *37*(4), 459–478.
Sullivan, A. (2002). Bourdieu and education: How useful is Bourdieu's theory for researchers? *The Netherlands' Journal of Social Sciences*, *38*(2), 144–166.
The Economic Times. (2014, October 27). *Lava to soon shift manufacturing base from China to India*. Retrieved August 23, 2017, from http://economictimes.indiatimes.com/tech/hardware/lava-to-soon-shift-manufacturing-base-from-china-to-india/articleshow/44943590.cms?intenttarget=no
The Indian Express. (2014). *Defence projects get Rs 80,000 cr push from govt; six made-in-India submarines also on list*. Retrieved August 23, 2017, from http://indianexpress.com/article/india/india-others/centre-gives-nod-to-defence-projects-worth-rs-80000-cr/
The People's Linguistic Survey of India. (2017). *Indian language in diaspora*. Retrieved November 12, 2016, from www.peopleslinguisticsurvey.org/view-Languages.aspx?id=8
The Probe Team. (2001). *Public report on basic education in India*. New Delhi: Oxford University Press.
The Times of India. (2010, March 14). *Indiaspeak: English is our 2nd language*. Retrieved February 15, 2013, from http://articles.timesofindia.indiatimes.com/2010-03-14/india/28117934_1_second-language-speakers-urdu
The Times of India. (2012, January 31). *CBSE vision 2012*. Retrieved May 23, 2014, from http://timesofindia.indiatimes.com/home/education/news/CBSE-Vision-2012/articleshow/11697672.cms
The Times of India. (2014, May 20). *Grade system scores for CBSE students*. Retrieved May 23, 2014, from http://timesofindia.indiatimes.com/city/bangalore/Grade-system-scores-for-CBSE-students/articleshow/35356129.cms
Tully, M. (1997). English: An advantage to India? *English Language Teaching Journal*, *51*(2), 151–164.
Vaish, V. (2005). A peripherist view of English as a language of decolonization in post-colonial India. *Language Policy*, *4*, 187–206.
Vermani, R. C. (2000). *Colonialism and nationalism in India*. New Delhi: Gitanjali Publishing House.
Williams, T., and Carpenter, P. (1991). Private schooling and public achievement in Australia. *International Journal of Educational Research*, *15*, 411–431.
Weeger, M. A., and Pacis, D. (2012). *A comparison of two theories of learning – behaviorism and constructivism as applied to face-to-face and online learning*. Retrieved March 11, 2019, from www.g-casa.com/conferences/manila/papers/Weegar.pdf
Young, G. M. (1967). *Macaulay: Prose and poetry*. London: Hart-Davis.

For Product Safety Concerns and Information please contact our EU
representative GPSR@taylorandfrancis.com
Taylor & Francis Verlag GmbH, Kaufingerstraße 24, 80331 München, Germany

www.ingramcontent.com/pod-product-compliance
Ingram Content Group UK Ltd.
Pitfield, Milton Keynes, MK11 3LW, UK
UKHW022123190926
475702UK00013B/1612
* 9 7 8 0 3 6 7 6 5 5 0 3 7 *